THE PENGUIN CLASSICS

*

THE MOST RECENT VOLUMES

EINHARD and NOTKER THE STAMMERER
Two Lives of Charlemagne · Lewis Thorpe

SENECA
Letters from a Stoic · *Robin Campbell*

DANTE
La Vita Nuova · *Barbara Reynolds*

EXQUEMELIN
The Buccaneers of America · *Alexis Brown*

THE ODES OF PINDAR
C. M. Bowra

THE FOUR VOYAGES OF CHRISTOPHER COLUMBUS
J. M. Cohen

LAXDAELA SAGA
Magnus Magnusson and *Hermann Pálsson*

CICERO
Selected Political Speeches · *Michael Grant*

THE ALEXIAD OF ANNA COMNENA
E. R. A. Sewter

FIVE GERMAN TRAGEDIES
F. J. Lamport

3H2345

FLAUBERT
SENTIMENTAL EDUCATION

Translated by Robert Baldick

'I know nothing more noble,' wrote Flaubert, 'than the contemplation of the world.' His acceptance of all the realities of life (rather than his remorseless exposure of its illusions) principally recommends what many regard as a more mature work than *Madame Bovary*, if not the greatest French novel of the last century. In Robert Baldick's new translation of this story of a young man's romantic attachment to an older woman, the modern English reader can appreciate the accuracy, the artistry, and the insight with which Flaubert (1821–80) reconstructed in one masterpiece the very fibre of his times.

Also available
MADAME BOVARY

GUSTAVE FLAUBERT

Three Tales

TRANSLATED
WITH AN INTRODUCTION BY
ROBERT BALDICK

PENGUIN BOOKS
BALTIMORE · MARYLAND

Penguin Books Ltd, Harmondsworth, Middlesex, England
Penguin Books Inc., 7110 Ambassador Road, Baltimore, Maryland 21207, U.S.A.
Penguin Books Australia Ltd, Ringwood, Victoria, Australia

—

This translation first published 1961
Reprinted 1965, 1967, 1969

—

Copyright © Robert Baldick, 1961

—

Made and printed in Great Britain
by Hazell Watson & Viney Ltd
Aylesbury, Bucks
Set in Linotype Granjon

CONTENTS

INTRODUCTION   7

THREE TALES

A Simple Heart   17
The Legend of St Julian Hospitator   57
Herodias   89

INTRODUCTION

WHEN Flaubert began writing the *Three Tales*, in 1875, the world saw him as a famous, prosperous author in his early fifties, with every reason to feel content with life; but he saw himself as an old man, with failure and sorrow behind him and poverty and death not far ahead.

He had spent the greater part of his adult life in the solitude of his home at Croisset, near Rouen, shunning the world and its pleasures, partly because of the mysterious nervous disease which had struck him down as a young man, but largely because he preferred to devote his energies almost exclusively to literature. Yet his books had brought him little satisfaction, and though he pretended that he did not care how they were received, he was deeply hurt by the hostility and incomprehension shown by public and critics alike. He had been put on trial for committing an 'outrage to public morals and religion' with *Madame Bovary* (1857); and if the book had sold well it had been for the wrong reasons, while the profits had disappeared into the publisher's pocket. *Salammbô* (1862), his novel on ancient Carthage, had been condemned by the critics as tedious, by the clergy as pagan, and by the archaeologists as inaccurate. *Sentimental Education* (1869), which Flaubert regarded as his masterpiece, had been greeted with uncomprehending abuse and its author accused of cynical immorality. In 1874 the final version of his *Temptation of St Anthony* had been virtually ignored, while his play *The Candidate* had been taken off after four disastrous performances; and at present he was working on the devastating satire *Bouvard and Pécuchet*, which was even less likely to appeal to the public of his day.

He had other, more personal reasons to feel sad and appre-

hensive in 1875. Many of his old friends and comrades in arms
had died in recent years: first Louis Bouilhet and Sainte-Beuve,
then Jules Duplan and Jules de Goncourt, and finally Théophile
Gautier and Ernest Feydeau. In 1870 the Prussians had occupied Croisset, and Flaubert had been forced not only to leave
his house but also to run errands for the enemy troops. Less
than two years later his mother had died. And then, in April
1875, his niece's husband, a wood-merchant called Ernest
Commanville, had been threatened with bankruptcy. To save
the Commanvilles Flaubert had put his entire fortune at their
disposal, sold all his property at Deauville, and even reconciled
himself to the possibility of giving up Croisset. Yet it was at
this unhappy time that he wrote the work which cost him the
least effort, gave him the most pleasure, and won the greatest
acclaim of all his books.

The *Three Tales* are still generally regarded as his most
successful and most representative work, and this is not simply
because they were the last of his writings to be published before his death in 1880. They reveal, it is true, a mastery of style
acquired in the course of a lifetime's arduous labour, but
each tale is also as it were a quintessential abstract of one or
more of Flaubert's great novels.

Thus *A Simple Heart* appears to combine the underlying
tenderness of *Sentimental Education* with the style and setting
of *Madame Bovary*; and readers of the latter novel will be
quick to notice the points of resemblance between Homais
and Bourias, between Emma Bovary's reactions to the ball at
La Vaubyessard and Félicité's to the fair at Colleville, between
the cinematic technique used in the famous scene of the agri-
cultural show in *Madame Bovary* and the analagous but rather
subtler presentation of Félicité's death. Similarly *The Legend of
St Julian Hospitator* recalls the more ambitious but less successful *Temptation of St Anthony*, while *Herodias*, despite all Flaubert's efforts to distinguish it from his previous essay in

historical reconstruction, inevitably invites comparison with *Salammbô*.

That is not to say that the *Three Tales* are merely exercises in literary dehydration. On the contrary, each story, for all its affinities with Flaubert's earlier work, has its separate origins in some aspect of his artistic or emotional experience.

This is even true of *Herodias*, which at first sight would seem to be the least personal of the three tales. It was almost certainly inspired by a sculptured tympanum on the front of the Cathedral at Rouen, the city where Flaubert was born in 1821 and where he spent his formative years, for on this tympanum the thirteenth-century sculptor represented Salome dancing on her hands in front of Herod, exactly as the nineteenth-century writer was to describe her in his story. But Flaubert had seen his Salome more than once in the flesh as well as in stone. In 1864, for instance, while taking a bath at an establishment in Corbeil, he had glimpsed her bare arm reaching through the half-open door of his cubicle to take his discarded clothes. And earlier still, in 1850, at Isna on the Middle Nile, Salome had danced for him in the person of Kuchiuk-Hanem, a lovely *almeh* from Cairo who performed the erotic Dance of the Bee to the sound of harps played by two blindfold musicians.

The Legend of St Julian Hospitator likewise owes something to Rouen Cathedral – this time to a stained-glass window in the north aisle which depicts the life of the Saint in some thirty scenes – though the idea of writing the story apparently came to Flaubert in 1846, when he and Maxime du Camp saw a little statue of St Julian in the church of Caudebec-en-Caux.

However, the story most closely associated with Flaubert's own life and with his native province is undoubtedly *A Simple Heart*. Every character, every place, every emotion in this tale corresponds to some person, some scene, some feeling in the author's past. In his childhood and youth he had often spent the summer holidays with his mother's relatives at Pont-l'Évêque or Trouville. All the place-names and descriptions given in *A Simple Heart* are accurate; several of the sites mentioned, such as the Marais and the farm of Geffosses, belonged to the Flauberts, and there was in fact a Golden Lamb at Trouville kept by a Mère David. As for the other minor figures in the story, Flaubert had either known them personally or heard his parents speak of them, and generally he alters their names only slightly, if at all; thus Pont-l'Évêque boasted a Bourais, a Varin, and a Mathieu, Nastasie Barette was a woman called La Barbette, while the disreputable Marquis de Grémanville was a no less disreputable great-uncle of Flaubert's, Fouet de Crémanville. Félicité herself was drawn partly from an unmarried mother called Léonie whom Flaubert had met at Trouville, and partly from Julie, the old servant who had been with his family since he was a boy and who was to outlive her master. Félicité's parrot belonged in reality to Pierre Barbey, a retired sea-captain living at Trouville, though Barbey's bird had a rather more extensive and colourful repertory of phrases than Loulou. Mme Aubain, Félicité's mistress, bears a strong resemblance to Flaubert's aunt, Mme Allais, who likewise lived for many years at Pont-l'Évêque. Her children, Paul and Virginie, are obviously Flaubert himself and his sister Caroline, whose early death caused Mme Flaubert the same overwhelming grief experienced by Mme Aubain. That does not mean that Paul Aubain is the only character to partake of the author. Indeed Flaubert appears to identify himself with a number of characters to the extent of endowing them with his own feelings and experiences down to the smallest details. Thus when he tells us that Mme Aubain had to sell most of her property and leave her house at Saint-Melaine for one at Pont-l'Évêque which was cheaper to run, we recall that he had recently been obliged to sell his land at Deauville and was preparing to give up his flat in the Rue Murillo in Paris to move into his niece's more modest apartment in the Faubourg Saint-Honoré. When we read that Félicité and Mme Aubain wept over Virginie's little moth-eaten plush hat, we are reminded that Flaubert treasured an old hat that had belonged to his mother. Most significant of all, when we are told how Félicité was struck down by the driver of a coach on the Honfleur road beyond Saint-Gatien, we remember that it was on this very same spot that Flaubert had suffered the first unexpected attack of his nervous disease in January 1844. For one brief moment at least, Flaubert and Félicité are joined together in an identical experience.

The actual writing of the *Three Tales* was begun in the autumn of 1875, while Flaubert was spending a peaceful holiday at Concarneau in Britanny with his friend Georges Pouchet, the natural historian. In a letter to Mme Roger des Genettes he explained that he had put *Bouvard and Pécuchet* aside for the moment and was looking for a more congenial subject for a novel. 'In the meantime,' he added, 'I am going to start writing *The Legend of St Julian Hospitator*, just to have something to do and to see if I am still capable of putting a sentence together, which I rather doubt.' In fact, as we have seen, the idea of writing the story of St Julian had come to him some thirty years before, and as recently as 1874 he had made copious notes on every aspect of hunting, an art on which his friend Edmond Laporte also gave him detailed information. For the account of the Saint's life he consulted various works of hagiography, notably the Bollandists, Jacopo da Voragine's *Golden Legend*, and one of the manuscripts of the thirteenth-century *Legend of St Julian* kept in the Bibliothèque Nationale, as well as the *Historical and Descriptive Essay on Glass Painting* by his old drawing-master, E. H. Langlois, a book which contained a reproduction of the Rouen Cathedral window. But in dealing with all these documents he exercised the artist's right to select, compress, and alter his material, deciding for instance that his Julian should discover the nature of his crime by himself and not from his wife, that he should leave his wife after the murder instead of travelling with her, and that instead of preceding him the Leper should carry him up to Heaven in a final apotheosis. In his correspondence Flaubert repeatedly and rightly emphasized the gulf which separated his sources from his finished work. Thus he claimed with justifiable complacency that no one would dare to compare the two nightmarish hunts in his story with the hunt in Victor Hugo's *Legend of the Handsome Pecopin*. And when a *de luxe* edition of his work was mooted some time later, Flaubert refused to authorize any illustration apart from a reproduction of the Rouen window – and that not because it could add anything to the story, but on the contrary because it would reveal the full extent of his achievement. To his uncomprehending publisher he wrote: 'Comparing the picture and the text, people would have said to themselves: "I don't understand. How did he get this from that?'

The Legend of St Julian Hospitator was completed in Paris in February 1876, and in March, saddened by the news of the death of Louise Colet, his former mistress, he set to work on *A Simple Heart*. The beginning of the story gave him considerable trouble: after working sixteen hours one day and all the next he found he had written only a single page. Then in April he paid a visit to Honfleur and Pont-l'Évêque which, as he told a friend, 'filled me with sadness, for I was obliged to steep myself in a bath of memories. How old I am, *mon Dieu*, how old!' He was writing this second tale especially for one of his dearest friends, George Sand, who had recently reproached him for 'spreading unhappiness' with his books, to show her that he was capable of telling a tender, moving story in a detached, unemotional style. But although George Sand had the pleasure of knowing that she had inspired *A Simple Heart*, she never read the story of Félicité. In June 1876 she died at her home at Nohant, where Flaubert attended her funeral, weep-

ing like a child at the sight of her coffin and feeling, as he later
told Maurice Sand, 'as if I were burying my mother for a second time'. He returned to Croisset to learn of the death of his
oldest childhood friend, Ernest Lemarié, and to complete *A
Simple Heart* in an atmosphere of nostalgic melancholy. Because the story owed so much to private memories, he was
even more than usually careful to guard against any possible
inaccuracy. Thus he consulted Grisolle's classic treatise on
pneumonia to describe Félicité's last illness, studied the Lisieux
euchology to get the details of the Corpus Christi procession
right, and even borrowed a stuffed parrot from Rouen Mus-
eum to serve as a model for Loulou. But this bird, installed in
a place of honour on Flaubert's work-table, like Loulou in
Félicité's bedroom, was more than just a visual aid : it was
another significant symbol of the link between author and
character.

From *A Simple Heart* Flaubert turned in August 1876 to
Herodias, a story inspired, as we have seen, partly by the
Rouen tympanum and partly no doubt by the author's incur-
able nostalgia for the East. He also had certain historical and
ethnological reasons for writing it, as he explained to Mme
Roger des Genettes. 'The story of Herodias,' he declared, 'as
I understand it, has nothing to do with religion. What attracts
me about it is the official attitude of Herod (who was a real
Prefect) and the ferocious figure of Herodias, a sort of cross
between Cleopatra and Mme de Maintenon. The racial question dominated everything.' Before he started writing *Herodias*, he consulted all the relevant sources, ancient and modern,
from the Gospels and Flavius Josephus down to Renan and
Parent. He begged the Orientalist Clermont-Ganneau for details of the view from the fortress of Machaerus; he asked his
friends Baudry and Laporte for the Arabic names of the stars
visible in Palestine towards the end of August; at one point he
even expressed regret that he could not have a newly severed

head before him when describing Salome's prize. By November 1876 the writing of *Herodias* was under way, in February 1877 it was completed, and in April the *Three Tales* were published in Paris by Charpentier.

Friends and critics promptly acclaimed the book as a masterpiece, the only dissenter of note being the implacable Brunetière, who expressed the opinion that it was 'the feeblest thing M. Flaubert has written to date'. A few attempts were made to link the tales together, either by regarding them as studies of three *illuminati* who found fulfilment in their different spheres, or by considering them as accounts of human activity in its historical, legendary, and everyday aspects. Most commentators, however, preferred to discuss each story separately.

Herodias was and still is the least admired of the three tales. Perhaps only a historian can do full justice to Flaubert's evocatory skill, and probably no tribute gave greater pleasure to the author than Taine's comment: 'These eighty pages teach me more about the circumstances, the origins, and the background of Christianity than all Renan's work.'

The Legend of St Julian Hospitator met with readier and warmer appreciation. It was generally acknowledged that the two-dimensional figures, the rich colours, the swift-moving action, the miraculous events, and the stylized descriptions all combined to produce the same effect as a stained-glass window or a Book of Hours. This, as Taine pointed out, was 'the world imagined by the Middle Ages and not the Middle Ages themselves'. On the other hand, Jules Lemaître, who described the story as 'a Gothic jewel of rare perfection', claimed that Flaubert had succeeded in capturing the essential spirit of medieval times. 'I consider this legend to be true', he wrote, 'in that Julian the parricide and the saint, with his lust for blood and his love of God, is wonderfully symbolic of the Middle Ages, their violence and their mysticism.'

It was *A Simple Heart*, however, which right from the start won the greatest acclaim. This was natural enough, for it was neither a historical reconstruction nor an artistic *tour de force* but a tale rooted in the author's own time and country, his own feelings and experiences. Here Flaubert had taken George Sand's advice and revealed something of his essential kindliness and gentleness, though not openly or explicitly. As the perceptive Jules Lemaître observed, 'Flaubert's style has never been more concise and controlled; one would think he was afraid of falling a prey to emotion'. Some critics have suggested that Flaubert's reference to 'dog-like devotion' shows contempt for Félicité, and that the final confusion in her mind between the stuffed parrot and the Holy Ghost is a stroke of cruel irony on the author's part. His close identification of himself with Félicité, to which we have already referred, would seem to contradict these hypotheses. But perhaps the last word on this point should be left to Flaubert himself.

'The *Story of a Simple Heart*', he told Mme Roger des Genettes, 'is just the account of an obscure life, that of a poor country girl, pious but fervent, discreetly loyal, and tender as new-baked bread. She loves one after the other a man, her mistress's children, a nephew of hers, an old man whom she nurses, and her parrot. When the parrot dies she has it stuffed, and when she herself comes to die she confuses the parrot with the Holy Ghost. This is not at all ironical as you may suppose, but on the contrary very serious and very sad. I want to move tender hearts to pity and tears, for I am tender-hearted myself.'

And the most deliberately impassive of all writers added hopefully: 'Now, surely, no one will accuse me of being inhuman any more....'

R. B.

A Simple Heart

I

FOR half a century the women of Pont-l'Évêque envied Mme Aubain her maidservant Félicité.

In return for a hundred francs a year she did all the cooking and the housework, the sewing, the washing, and the ironing. She could bridle a horse, fatten poultry, and churn butter, and she remained faithful to her mistress, who was by no means an easy person to get on with.

Mme Aubain had married a young fellow who was good-looking but badly-off, and who died at the beginning of 1809, leaving her with two small children and a pile of debts. She then sold all her property except for the farms of Toucques and Geffosses, which together brought in five thousand francs a year at the most, and left her house at Saint-Melaine for one behind the covered market which was cheaper to run and had belonged to her family.

This house had a slate roof and stood between an alley-way and a lane leading down to the river. Inside there were differences in level which were the cause of many a stumble. A narrow entrance-hall separated the kitchen from the parlour, where Mme Aubain sat all day long in a wicker easy-chair by the window. Eight mahogany chairs were lined up against the white-painted wainscoting, and under the barometer stood an old piano loaded with a pyramid of boxes and cartons. On either side of the chimney-piece, which was carved out of yellow marble in the Louis Quinze style, there was a tapestry-covered arm-chair, and in the middle was a clock designed to look like a temple of Vesta. The whole room smelt a little musty, as the floor was on a lower level than the garden.

On the first floor was 'Madame's' bedroom – very spacious, with a patterned wallpaper of pale flowers and a portrait of 'Monsieur' dressed in what had once been the height of fashion. It opened into a smaller room in which there were two cots, without mattresses. Then came the drawing-room, which was always shut up and full of furniture covered with dustsheets. Next there was a passage leading to the study, where books and papers filled the shelves of a book-case in three sections built round a big writing-table of dark wood. The two end panels were hidden under pen-and-ink drawings, landscapes in gouache, and etchings by Audran, souvenirs of better days and bygone luxury. On the second floor a dormer window gave light to Félicité's room, which looked out over the fields.

Every day Félicité got up at dawn, so as not to miss Mass, and worked until evening without stopping. Then, once dinner was over, the plates and dishes put away, and the door bolted, she piled ashes on the log fire and went to sleep in front of the hearth, with her rosary in her hands. Nobody could be more stubborn when it came to haggling over prices, and as for cleanliness, the shine on her saucepans was the despair of all the other servants. Being of a thrifty nature, she ate slowly, picking up from the table the crumbs from her loaf of bread – a twelve-pound loaf which was baked specially for her and lasted her twenty days.

All the year round she wore a kerchief of printed calico fastened behind with a pin, a bonnet which covered her hair, grey stockings, a red skirt, and over her jacket a bibbed apron such as hospital nurses wear.

Her face was thin and her voice was sharp. At twenty-five she was often taken for forty; once she reached fifty, she stopped looking any age in particular. Always silent and upright and deliberate in her movements, she looked like a wooden doll driven by clock-work.

2

LIKE everyone else, she had had her love-story.

Her father, a mason, had been killed when he fell off some scaffolding. Then her mother died, and when her sisters went their separate ways, a farmer took her in, sending her, small as she was, to look after the cows out in the fields. She went about in rags, shivering with cold, used to lie flat on the ground to drink water out of the ponds, would be beaten for no reason at all, and was finally turned out of the house for stealing thirty sous, a theft of which she was innocent. She found work at another farm, looking after the poultry, and as she was liked by her employers the other servants were jealous of her.

One August evening – she was eighteen at the time – they took her off to the fête at Colleville. From the start she was dazed and bewildered by the noise of the fiddles, the lamps in the trees, the medley of gaily coloured dresses, the gold crosses and lace, and the throng of people jigging up and down. She was standing shyly on one side when a smart young fellow, who had been leaning on the shaft of a cart, smoking his pipe, came up and asked her to dance. He treated her to cider, coffee, girdle-cake, and a silk neckerchief, and imagining that she knew what he was after, offered to see her home. At the edge of a field of oats, he pushed her roughly to the ground. Thoroughly frightened, she started screaming for help. He took to his heels.

Another night, on the road to Beaumont, she tried to get past a big, slow-moving waggon loaded with hay, and as she was squeezing by she recognized Théodore.

He greeted her quite calmly, saying that she must forgive him for the way he had behaved to her, as 'it was the drink that did it'.

She did not know what to say in reply and felt like running off.

Straight away he began talking about the crops and the notabilities of the commune, saying that his father had left Colleville for the farm at Les Écots, so that they were now neighbours.

'Ah!' she said.

He added that his family wanted to see him settled but that he was in no hurry and was waiting to find a wife to suit his fancy. She lowered her head. Then he asked her if she was thinking of getting married. She answered with a smile that it was mean of him to make fun of her.

'But I'm not making fun of you!' he said. 'I swear I'm not!'

He put his left arm round her waist, and she walked on supported by his embrace. Soon they slowed down. There was a gentle breeze blowing, the stars were shining, the huge load of hay was swaying about in front of them, and the four horses were raising clouds of dust as they shambled along. Then, without being told, they turned off to the right. He kissed her once more and she disappeared into the darkness.

The following week Théodore got her to grant him several rendezvous.

They would meet at the bottom of a farm-yard, behind a wall, under a solitary tree. She was not ignorant of life as young ladies are, for the animals had taught her a great deal; but her reason and an instinctive sense of honour prevented her from giving way. The resistance she put up inflamed Théodore's passion to such an extent that in order to satisfy it (or perhaps out of sheer naïvety) he proposed to her. At first she refused to believe him, but he swore that he was serious.

Soon afterwards he had a disturbing piece of news to tell her: the year before, his parents had paid a man to do his military service for him, but now he might be called up again any day, and the idea of going into the army frightened him.

In Félicité's eyes this cowardice of his appeared to be a proof of his affection, and she loved him all the more for it. Every night she would steal out to meet him, and every night Théodore would plague her with his worries and entreaties.

In the end he said that he was going to the Prefecture himself to make inquiries, and that he would come and tell her how matters stood the following Sunday, between eleven and midnight.

At the appointed hour she hurried to meet her sweetheart, but found one of his friends waiting for her instead.

He told her that she would not see Théodore again. To make sure of avoiding conscription, he had married a very rich old woman, Mme Lehoussais of Toucques.

Her reaction was an outburst of frenzied grief. She threw herself on the ground, screaming and calling on God, and lay moaning all alone in the open until sunrise. Then she went back to the farm and announced her intention of leaving. At the end of the month, when she had received her wages, she wrapped her small belongings up in a kerchief and made her way to Pont-l'Évêque.

In front of the inn there, she sought information from a woman in a widow's bonnet, who, as it happened, was looking for a cook. The girl did not know much about cooking, but she seemed so willing and expected so little that finally Mme Aubain ended up by saying: 'Very well, I will take you on.'

A quarter of an hour later Félicité was installed in her house.

At first she lived there in a kind of fearful awe caused by 'the style of the house' and by the memory of 'Monsieur' brooding over everything. Paul and Virginie, the boy aged seven and the girl barely four, seemed to her to be made of some precious substance. She used to carry them about pick-a-back, and when Mme Aubain told her not to keep on kissing them she was cut to the quick. All the same, she was happy now, for her pleasant surroundings had dispelled her grief.

On Thursdays, a few regular visitors came in to play Boston, and Félicité got the cards and the footwarmers ready beforehand. They always arrived punctually at eight, and left before the clock struck eleven.

Every Monday morning the second-hand dealer who lived down the alley put all his junk out on the pavement. Then the hum of voices began to fill the town, mingled with the neighing of horses, the bleating of lambs, the grunting of pigs, and the rattle of carts in the streets.

About midday, when the market was in full swing, a tall old peasant with a hooked nose and his cap on the back of his head would appear at the door. This was Robelin, the farmer from Geffosses. A little later, and Liébard, the farmer from Toucques, would arrive – a short, fat, red-faced fellow in a grey jacket and leather gaiters fitted with spurs.

Both men had hens or cheeses they wanted to sell to 'Madame'. But Félicité was up to all their tricks and invariably outwitted them, so that they went away full of respect for her.

From time to time Mme Aubain had a visit from an uncle of hers, the Marquis de Grémanville, who had been ruined by loose living and was now living at Falaise on his last remaining scrap of property. He always turned up at lunch-time, accompanied by a hideous poodle which dirtied all the furniture with its paws. However hard he tried to behave like a gentleman, even going so far as to raise his hat every time he mentioned 'my late father', the force of habit was usually too much for him, for he would start pouring himself one glass after another and telling bawdy stories. Félicité used to push him gently out of the house, saying politely: 'You've had quite enough, Monsieur de Grémanville. See you another time!' and shutting the door on him.

She used to open it with pleasure to M. Bourais, who was a retired solicitor. His white tie and his bald head, his frilled shirt-front and his ample brown frock-coat, the way he had of rounding his arm to take a pinch of snuff, and indeed everything about him made an overwhelming impression on her such as we feel when we meet some outstanding personality.

As he looked after 'Madame's' property, he used to shut himself up with her for hours in 'Monsieur's' study. He lived in dread of compromising his reputation, had a tremendous respect for the Bench, and laid claim to some knowledge of Latin.

To give the children a little painless instruction, he made them a present of a geography book with illustrations. These represented scenes in different parts of the world, such as cannibals wearing feather head-dresses, a monkey carrying off a young lady, Bedouins in the desert, a whale being harpooned, and so on.

Paul explained these pictures to Félicité, and that indeed was all the education she ever had. As for the children, they were taught by Guyot, a poor devil employed at the Town Hall, who was famous for his beautiful handwriting, and who had a habit of sharpening his penknife on his boots.

When the weather was fine the whole household used to set off early for a day at the Geffosses farm.

The farm-yard there was on a slope, with the house in the middle; and the sea, in the distance, looked like a streak of grey. Félicité would take some slices of cold meat out of her basket, and they would have their lunch in a room adjoining the dairy. It was all that remained of a country house which had fallen into ruin, and the wallpaper hung in shreds, fluttering in the draught. Mme Aubain used to sit with bowed head, absorbed in her memories, so that the children were afraid to talk. 'Why don't you run along and play?' she would say, and away they went.

Paul climbed up into the barn, caught birds, played ducks and drakes on the pond, or banged with a stick on the great casks, which sounded just like drums.

Virginie fed the rabbits, or scampered off to pick cornflowers, showing her little embroidered knickers as she ran.

One autumn evening they came home through the fields. The moon, which was in its first quarter, lit up part of the sky, and there was some mist floating like a scarf over the winding Toucques. The cattle, lying out in the middle of the pasture, looked peacefully at the four people walking by. In the third field a few got up and made a half circle in front of them.

'Don't be frightened!' said Félicité, and crooning softly, she stroked the back of the nearest animal. It turned about and the others did the same. But while they were crossing the next field they suddenly heard a dreadful bellowing. It came from a bull which had been hidden by the mist, and which now came towards the two women.

Mme Aubain started to run.

'No! No!' said Félicité. 'Not so fast!'

All the same they quickened their pace, hearing behind them a sound of heavy breathing which came nearer and nearer. The bull's hooves thudded like hammers on the turf, and they realized that it had broken into a gallop. Turning round, Félicité tore up some clods of earth and flung them at its eyes. It lowered its muzzle and thrust its horns forward, trembling with rage and bellowing horribly.

By now Mme Aubain had got to the end of the field with her two children and was frantically looking for a way over the high bank. Félicité was still backing away from the bull, hurling clods of turf which blinded it, and shouting: 'Hurry! Hurry!'

Mme Aubain got down into the ditch, pushed first Virginie and then Paul up the other side, fell once or twice trying to climb the bank, and finally managed it with a valiant effort.

The bull had driven Félicité back against a gate, and its slaver was spurting into her face. In another second it would have gored her, but she just had time to slip between two of the bars, and the great beast halted in amazement.

This adventure was talked about at Pont-l'Évêque for a good many years, but Félicité never prided herself in the least on what she had done, as it never occurred to her that she had done anything heroic.

Virginie claimed all her attention, for the fright had affected the little girl's nerves, and M. Poupart, the doctor, recommended sea-bathing at Trouville.

In those days the resort had few visitors. Mme Aubain made inquiries, consulted Bourais, and got everything ready as though for a long journey.

Her luggage went off in Liébard's cart the day before she left. The next morning he brought along two horses, one of which had a woman's saddle with a velvet back, while the other carried a cloak rolled up to make a kind of seat on its crupper. Mme Aubain sat on this, with Liébard in front. Félicité looked after Virginie on the other horse, and Paul mounted M. Lechaptois's donkey, which he had lent them on condition they took great care of it.

The road was so bad that it took two hours to travel the five miles to Toucques. The horses sank into the mud up to their pasterns and had to jerk their hind-quarters to get out; often they stumbled in the ruts, or else they had to jump. In some places, Liébard's mare came to a sudden stop, and while he waited patiently for her to move off again, he talked about the people whose properties bordered the road, adding moral reflexions to each story. For instance, in the middle of Toucques, as they were passing underneath some windows set in a mass of nasturtiums, he shrugged his shoulders and said:

'There's a Madame Lehoussais lives here. Now instead of taking a young man, she . . .'

Félicité did not hear the rest, for the horses had broken into a trot and the donkey was galloping along. All three turned down a bridle-path, a gate swung open, a couple of boys appeared, and everyone dismounted in front of a manure-heap right outside the farm-house door.

Old Mother Liébard welcomed her mistress with every appearance of pleasure. She served up a sirloin of beef for lunch, with tripe and black pudding, a fricassee of chicken, sparkling cider, a fruit tart and brandy-plums, garnishing the whole meal with compliments to Madame, who seemed to be enjoying better health, to Mademoiselle, who had turned into a 'proper little beauty', and to Monsieur Paul, who had 'filled out a lot'. Nor did she forget their deceased grand-parents, whom the Liébards had known personally, having been in the family's service for several generations.

Like its occupants, the farm had an air of antiquity. The ceiling-beams were worm-eaten, the walls black with smoke, and the window-panes grey with dust. There was an oak dresser laden with all sorts of odds and ends – jugs, plates, pewter bowls, wolf-traps, sheep-shears, and an enormous syringe which amused the children. In the three yards outside there was not a single tree without either mushrooms at its base or mistletoe in its branches. Several had been blown down and had taken root again at the middle; all of them were bent under the weight of their apples. The thatched roofs, which looked like brown velvet and varied in thickness, weathered the fiercest winds, but the cart-shed was tumbling down. Mme Aubain said that she would have it seen to, and ordered the animals to be reharnessed.

It took them another half-hour to reach Trouville. The little caravan dismounted to make their way along the Écores, a cliff jutting right out over the boats moored below; and three minutes later they got to the end of the quay and entered the courtyard of the Golden Lamb, the inn kept by Mère David.

After the first few days Virginie felt stronger, as a result of the change of air and the sea-bathing. Not having a costume, she went into the water in her chemise and her maid dressed her afterwards in a customs officer's hut which was used by the bathers.

In the afternoons they took the donkey and went off beyond the Roches-Noires, in the direction of Hennequeville. To begin with, the path went uphill between gentle slopes like the lawns in a park, and then came out on a plateau where pasture-land and ploughed fields alternated. On either side there were holly-bushes standing out from the tangle of brambles, and here and there a big dead tree spread its zigzag branches against the blue sky.

They almost always rested in the same field, with Deauville on their left, Le Havre on their right, and the open sea in front. The water glittered in the sunshine, smooth as a mirror, and so still that the murmur it made was scarcely audible; unseen sparrows could be heard twittering, and the sky covered the whole scene with its huge canopy. Mme Aubain sat doing her needlework, Virginie plaited rushes beside her, Félicité gathered lavender, and Paul, feeling profoundly bored, longed to get up and go.

Sometimes they crossed the Toucques in a boat and hunted for shells. When the tide went out, sea-urchins, ormers, and jelly-fish were left behind; and the children scampered around, snatching at the foam-flakes carried on the wind. The sleepy waves, breaking on the sand, spread themselves out along the shore. The beach stretched as far as the eye could see, bounded on the land side by the dunes which separated it from the Marais, a broad meadow in the shape of an arena. When they came back that way, Trouville, on the distant hillside, grew bigger at every step, and with its medley of oddly assorted houses seemed to blossom out in gay disorder.

On exceptionally hot days they stayed in their room. The

sun shone in dazzling bars of light between the slats of the blind. There was not a sound to be heard in the village, and not a soul to be seen down in the street. Everything seemed more peaceful in the prevailing silence. In the distance caulkers were hammering away at the boats, and the smell of tar was wafted along by a sluggish breeze.

The principal amusement consisted in watching the fishing-boats come in. As soon as they had passed the buoys, they started tacking. With their canvas partly lowered and their foresails blown out like balloons they glided through the splashing waves as far as the middle of the harbour, where they suddenly dropped anchor. Then each boat came alongside the quay, and the crew threw ashore their catch of quivering fish. A line of carts stood waiting, and women in cotton bonnets rushed forward to take the baskets and kiss their men.

One day one of these women spoke to Félicité, who came back to the inn soon after in a state of great excitement. She explained that she had found one of her sisters – and Nastasie Barette, now Leroux, made her appearance, with a baby at her breast, another child holding her right hand, and on her left a little sailor-boy, his arms akimbo and his cap over one ear.

Mme Aubain sent her off after a quarter of an hour. From then on they were forever hanging round the kitchen or loitering about when the family went for a walk, though the husband kept out of sight.

Félicité became quite attached to them. She bought them a blanket, several shirts, and a stove; and it was clear that they were bent on getting all they could out of her.

This weakness of hers annoyed Mme Aubain, who in any event disliked the familiar way in which the nephew spoke to Paul. And so, as Virginie had started coughing and the good weather was over, she decided to go back to Pont-l'Évêque.

M. Bourais advised her on the choice of a school; Caen was

considered the best, so it was there that Paul was sent. He said good-bye bravely, feeling really rather pleased to be going to a place where he would have friends of his own.

Mme Aubain resigned herself to the loss of her son, knowing that it was unavoidable. Virginie soon got used to it. Félicité missed the din he used to make, but she was given something new to do which served as a distraction: from Christmas onwards she had to take the little girl to catechism every day.

3

AFTER genuflecting at the door, she walked up the centre aisle under the nave, opened the door of Mme Aubain's pew, sat down, and started looking about her.

The choir stalls were all occupied, with the boys on the right and the girls on the left, while the curé stood by the lectern. In one of the stained-glass windows in the apse the Holy Ghost looked down on the Virgin; another window showed her kneeling before the Infant Jesus; and behind the tabernacle there was a wood-carving of St Michael slaying the dragon.

The priest began with a brief outline of sacred history. Listening to him, Félicité saw in imagination the Garden of Eden, the Flood, the Tower of Babel, cities burning, peoples dying, and idols being overthrown; and this dazzling vision left her with a great respect for the Almighty and profound fear of His wrath.

Then she wept as she listened to the story of the Passion. Why had they crucified Him, when He loved children, fed the multitudes, healed the blind, and had chosen out of humility to be born among the poor, on the litter of a stable? The sowing of the seed, the reaping of the harvest, the pressing of the grapes – all those familiar things of which the Gospels speak had their place in her life. God had sanctified them in passing, so that she loved the lambs more tenderly for love of the Lamb of God, and the doves for the sake of the Holy Ghost.

She found it difficult, however, to imagine what the Holy Ghost looked like, for it was not just a bird but a fire as well, and sometimes a breath. She wondered whether that was its light she had seen flitting about the edge of the marshes at night, whether that was its breath she had felt driving the clouds across the sky, whether that was its voice she had heard in the sweet music of the bells. And she sat in silent adoration, delighting in the coolness of the walls and the quiet of the church.

Of dogma she neither understood nor even tried to understand anything. The curé discoursed, the children repeated their lesson, and she finally dropped off to sleep, waking up suddenly at the sound of their sabots clattering across the flagstones as they left the church.

It was in this manner, simply by hearing it expounded, that she learnt her catechism, for her religious education had been neglected in her youth. From then on she copied all Virginie's observances, fasting when she did and going to confession with her. On the feast of Corpus Christi the two of them made an altar of repose together.

The preparations for Virginie's first communion caused her great anxiety. She worried over her shoes, her rosary, her missal, and her gloves. And how she trembled as she helped Mme Aubain to dress the child!

All through the Mass her heart was in her mouth. One side of the choir was hidden from her by M. Bourais, but directly opposite her she could see the flock of maidens, looking like a field of snow with their white crowns perched on top of their veils; and she recognized her little darling from a distance by her dainty neck and her rapt attitude. The bell tinkled. Every head bowed low, and there was a silence. Then, to the thunderous accompaniment of the organ, choir and congregation joined in singing the *Agnus Dei*. Next the boys' procession began, and after that the girls got up from their seats. Slowly, their hands joined in prayer, they went towards the brightly lit altar, knelt on the first step, received the Host one by one, and went back to their places in the same order. When it was Virginie's turn, Félicité leant forward to see her, and in one of those imaginative flights born of real affection, it seemed to her that she herself was in the child's place. Virginie's face became her own, Virginie's dress clothed her, Virginie's heart was beating in her breast; and as she closed her eyes and opened her mouth, she almost fainted away.

Early next morning she went to the sacristy and asked M. le Curé to give her communion. She received the sacrament with all due reverence, but did not feel the same rapture as she had the day before.

Mme Aubain wanted her daughter to possess every accomplishment, and since Guyot could not teach her English or music, she decided to send her as a boarder to the Ursuline Convent at Honfleur.

Virginie raised no objection, but Félicité went about sighing at Madame's lack of feeling. Then she thought that perhaps her mistress was right: such matters, after all, lay outside her province.

Finally the day arrived when an old waggonette stopped at their door, and a nun got down from it who had come to fetch Mademoiselle. Félicité hoisted the luggage up on top, gave the driver some parting instructions, and put six pots of jam, a dozen pears, and a bunch of violets in the boot.

At the last moment Virginie burst into a fit of sobbing. She threw her arms round her mother, who kissed her on the forehead, saying: 'Come now, be brave, be brave.' The step was pulled up and the carriage drove away.

Then Mme Aubain broke down, and that evening all her friends, M. and Mme Lormeau, Mme Lechaptois, the Rochefeuille sisters, M. de Houppeville, and Bourais, came in to console her.

To begin with she missed her daughter badly. But she had a letter from her three times a week, wrote back on the other days, walked round her garden, did a little reading, and thus contrived to fill the empty hours.

As for Félicité, she went into Virginie's room every morning from sheer force of habit and looked round it. It upset her not having to brush the child's hair any more, tie her bootlaces, or tuck her up in bed; and she missed seeing her sweet face all the time and holding her hand when they went out together. For want of something to do, she tried making lace, but her fingers were too clumsy and broke the threads. She could not settle to anything, lost her sleep, and, to use her own words, was 'eaten up inside'.

To 'occupy her mind', she asked if her nephew Victor might come and see her, and permission was granted.

He used to arrive after Mass on Sunday, his cheeks flushed, his chest bare, and smelling of the countryside through which he had come. She laid a place for him straight away, opposite hers, and they had lunch together. Eating as little as possible herself, in order to save the expense, she stuffed him so full of food that he fell asleep after the meal. When the first bell for vespers rang, she woke him up, brushed his trousers, tied his tie, and set off for church, leaning on his arm with all a mother's pride.

His parents always told him to get something out of her – a packet of brown sugar perhaps, some soap, or a little brandy, sometimes even money. He brought her his clothes to be mended, and she did the work gladly, thankful for anything that would force him to come again.

In August his father took him on a coasting trip. The child-

ren's holidays were just beginning, and it cheered her up to
have them home again. But Paul was turning capricious and
Virginie was getting too old to be addressed familiarly – a
state of affairs which put a barrier of constraint between them.

Victor went to Morlaix, Dunkirk, and Brighton in turn,
and brought her a present after each trip. The first time it was
a box covered with shells, the second a coffee cup, the third
a big gingerbread man. He was growing quite handsome, with
his trim figure, his little moustache, his frank open eyes, and
the little leather cap that he wore on the back of his head like a
pilot. He kept her amused by telling her stories full of nautical
jargon.

One Monday – it was the fourteenth of July 1819, a date
she never forgot – Victor told her that he had signed on for
an ocean voyage, and that on the Wednesday night he would
be taking the Honfleur packet to join his schooner, which was
due to sail shortly from Le Havre. He might be away, he said,
for two years.

The prospect of such a long absence made Félicité extremely
unhappy, and she felt she must bid him godspeed once more.
So on the Wednesday evening, when Madame's dinner was
over, she put on her clogs and swiftly covered the ten miles
between Pont-l'Évêque and Honfleur.

When she arrived at the Calvary she turned right instead of
left, got lost in the shipyards, and had to retrace her steps.
Some people she spoke to advised her to hurry. She went right
round the harbour, which was full of boats, constantly tripping
over moorings. Then the ground fell away, rays of light criss-
crossed in front of her, and for a moment she thought she was
going mad, for she could see horses up in the sky.

On the quayside more horses were neighing, frightened by
the sea. A derrick was hoisting them into the air and dropping
them into one of the boats, which was already crowded with
passengers elbowing their way between barrels of cider,

baskets of cheese, and sacks of grain. Hens were cackling and the captain swearing, while a cabin-boy stood leaning on the cats-head, completely indifferent to it all. Félicité, who had not recognized him, shouted: 'Victor!' and he raised his head. She rushed forward, but at that very moment the gangway was pulled ashore.

The packet moved out of the harbour with women singing as they hauled it along, its ribs creaking and heavy waves lashing its bows. The sail swung round, hiding everyone on board from view, and against the silvery, moonlit sea the boat appeared as a dark shape that grew ever fainter, until at last it vanished in the distance.

As Félicité was passing the Calvary, she felt a longing to commend to God's mercy all that she held most dear; and she stood there praying for a long time, her face bathed in tears, her eyes fixed upon the clouds. The town was asleep, except for the customs officers walking up and down. Water was pouring ceaselessly through the holes in the sluice-gate, making as much noise as a torrent. The clocks struck two.

The convent parlour would not be open before daybreak, and Madame would be annoyed if she were late; so, although she would have liked to give a kiss to the other child, she set off for home. The maids at the inn were just waking up as she got to Pont-l'Évêque.

So the poor lad was going to be tossed by the waves for months on end! His previous voyages had caused her no alarm. People came back from England and Brittany; but America, the Colonies, the Islands, were all so far away, somewhere at the other end of the world.

From then on Félicité thought of nothing but her nephew. On sunny days she hoped he was not too thirsty, and when there was a storm she was afraid he would be struck by lightning. Listening to the wind howling in the chimney or blowing slates off the roof, she saw him being buffeted by the very same storm, perched on the top of a broken mast, with his whole body bent backwards under a sheet of foam; or again – and these were reminiscences of the illustrated geography-book – he was being eaten by savages, captured by monkeys in a forest, or dying on a desert shore. But she never spoke of her worries.

Mme Aubain had worries of her own about her daughter. The good nuns said that she was an affectionate child, but very delicate. The slightest emotion upset her, and she had to give up playing the piano.

Her mother insisted on regular letters from the convent. One morning when the postman had not called, she lost patience and walked up and down the room, between her chair and the window. It was really extraordinary! Four days without any news!

Thinking her own example would comfort her, Félicité said:

'I've been six months, Madame, without news.'

'News of whom?'

The servant answered gently:

'Why – of my nephew.'

'Oh, your nephew!' And Mme Aubain started pacing up and down again, with a shrug of her shoulders that seemed to say: 'I wasn't thinking of him – and indeed, why should I? Who cares about a young, good-for-nothing cabin-boy? Whereas my daughter – why, just think!'

Although she had been brought up the hard way, Félicité was indignant with Madame, but she soon forgot. It struck her as perfectly natural to lose one's head where the little girl was concerned. For her, the two children were of equal importance; they were linked together in her heart by a single bond, and their destinies should be the same.

The chemist told her that Victor's ship had arrived at Havana: he had seen this piece of information in a newspaper.

Because of its association with cigars, she imagined Havana as a place where nobody did anything but smoke, and pictured Victor walking about among crowds of Negroes in a cloud of tobacco-smoke. Was it possible, she wondered, 'in case of need' to come back by land? And how far was it from Pontl'Évêque? To find out she asked M. Bourais.

He reached for his atlas, and launched forth into an explanation of latitudes and longitudes, smiling like the pedant he was at Félicité's bewilderment. Finally he pointed with his pencil at a minute black dot inside a ragged oval patch, saying:

'There it is.'

She bent over the map, but the network of coloured lines meant nothing to her and only tired her eyes. So when Bourais asked her to tell him what was puzzling her, she begged him to show her the house where Victor was living. He threw up his hands, sneezed, and roared with laughter, delighted to come across such simplicity. And Félicité – whose intelligence was so limited that she probably expected to see an actual portrait of her nephew – could not make out why he was laughing.

It was a fortnight later that Liébard came into the kitchen at market-time, as he usually did, and handed her a letter from her brother-in-law. As neither of them could read, she turned to her mistress for help.

Mme Aubain, who was counting the stitches in her knitting, put it down and unsealed the letter. She gave a start, and, looking hard at Félicité, said quietly:

'They have some bad news for you ... Your nephew ...'

He was dead. That was all the letter had to say.

Félicité dropped on to a chair, leaning her head against the wall and closing her eyelids, which suddenly turned pink. Then, with her head bowed, her hands dangling, and her eyes set, she kept repeating:

'Poor little lad! Poor little lad!'

Liébard looked at her and sighed. Mme Aubain was trembling slightly. She suggested that she should go and see her sister at Trouville, but Félicité shook her head to indicate that there was no need for that.

There was a silence. Old Liébard thought it advisable to go.

Then Félicité said:

'It doesn't matter a bit, not to them it doesn't.'

Her head fell forward again, and from time to time she unconsciously picked up the knitting needles lying on the worktable.

Some women went past carrying a tray full of dripping linen.

Catching sight of them through the window, she remembered her own washing; she had passed the lye through it the day before and today it needed rinsing. So she left the room.

Her board and tub were on the bank of the Touques. She threw a pile of chemises down by the water's edge, rolled up her sleeves, and picked up her battledore. The lusty blows she gave with it could be heard in all the neighbouring gardens.

The fields were empty, the river rippling in the wind; at the bottom long weeds were waving to and fro, like the hair of corpses floating in the water. She held back her grief, and was very brave until the evening; but in her room she gave way to it completely, lying on her mattress with her face buried in the pillow and her fists pressed against her temples.

Long afterwards she learnt the circumstances of Victor's death from the captain of his ship. He had gone down with yellow fever, and they had bled him too much at the hospital. Four doctors had held him at once. He had died straight away, and the chief doctor had said:

'Good! There goes another!'

His parents had always treated him cruelly. She preferred not to see them again, and they made no advances, either because they had forgotten about her or out of the callousness of the poor.

Meanwhile Virginie was growing weaker. Difficulty in breathing, fits of coughing, protracted bouts of fever, and mottled patches on the cheekbones all indicated some deep-seated complaint. M. Poupart had advised a stay in Provence. Mme Aubain decided to follow this suggestion, and, if it had not been for the weather at Pont-l'Évêque, she would have brought her daughter home at once.

She arranged with a jobmaster to drive her out to the convent every Tuesday. There was a terrace in the garden, overlooking the Seine, and there Virginie, leaning on her mother's arm, walked up and down over the fallen vine-leaves. Sometimes, while she was looking at the sails in the distance, or at the long stretch of horizon from the Château de Tancarville to the lighthouses of Le Havre, the sun would break through the clouds and make her blink. Afterwards they would rest in the arbour. Her mother had secured a little cask of excellent Malaga, and, laughing at the idea of getting tipsy, Virginie used to drink a thimbleful, but no more.

Her strength revived. Autumn slipped by, and Félicité assured Mme Aubain that there was nothing to fear. But one evening, coming back from some errand in the neighbour-hood, she found M. Poupart's gig standing at the door. He was in the hall, and Mme Aubain was tying on her bonnet.

'Give me my foot-warmer, purse, gloves. Quickly now!'

Virginie had pneumonia and was perhaps past recovery.

'Not yet!' said the doctor; and the two of them got into the carriage with snow-flakes swirling around them. Night was falling and it was very cold.

Félicité rushed into the church to light a candle, and then ran after the gig. She caught up with it an hour later, jumped lightly up behind, and hung on to the fringe. But then a thought struck her: the courtyard had not been locked up, and burglars might get in. So she jumped down again.

At dawn the next day she went to the doctor's. He had come home and gone out again on his rounds. Then she waited at the inn, thinking that somebody who was a stranger to the district might call there with a letter. Finally, when it was twilight, she got into the coach for Lisieux.

The convent was at the bottom of a steep lane. When she was half-way down the hill, she heard a strange sound which she recognized as a death-bell tolling.

'It's for somebody else', she thought, as she banged the door-knocker hard.

After a few minutes she heard the sound of shuffling feet, the door opened a little way, and a nun appeared.

The good sister said with an air of compunction that 'she had just passed away'. At that moment the bell of Saint-Léonard was tolled more vigorously than ever.

Félicité went up to the second floor. From the doorway of the room she could see Virginie lying on her back, her hands clasped together, her mouth open, her head tilted back under a black crucifix that leant over her, her face whiter than the curtains that hung motionless on either side. Mme Aubain was clinging to the foot of the bed and sobbing desperately. The Mother Superior stood on the right. Three candlesticks on the chest of drawers added touches of red to the scene, and fog was whitening the windows. Some nuns led Mme Aubain away.

For two nights Félicité never left the dead girl. She said the same prayers over and over again, sprinkled holy water on the sheets, then sat down again to watch. At the end of her first vigil, she noticed that the child's face had gone yellow, the lips were turning blue, the nose looked sharper, and the eyes were sunken. She kissed them several times, and would not have been particularly surprised if Virginie had opened them again: to minds like hers the supernatural is a simple matter.

She laid her out, wrapped her in a shroud, put her in her coffin, placed a wreath on her, and spread out her hair. It was fair and amazingly long for her age. Félicité cut off a big lock, half of which she slipped into her bosom, resolving never to part with it.

The body was brought back to Pont-l'Évêque at the request of Mme Aubain, who followed the hearse in a closed carriage.

After the Requiem Mass, it took another three-quarters of an hour to reach the cemetery. Paul walked in front, sobbing. Then came M. Bourais, and after him the principal inhabitants of the town, the women all wearing long black veils, and Félicité. She was thinking about her nephew; and since she had been unable to pay him these last honours, she felt an added grief, just as if they were burying him with Virginie.

Mme Aubain's despair passed all bounds. First of all she rebelled against God, considering it unfair of Him to have taken her daughter from her – for she had never done any harm, and her conscience was quite clear. But was it? She ought to have taken Virginie to the south; other doctors would have saved her life. She blamed herself, wished she could have joined her daughter, and cried out in anguish in her dreams. One dream in particular obsessed her. Her husband, dressed like a sailor, came back from a long voyage, and told her amid tears that he had been ordered to take Virginie away – whereupon they put their heads together to discover somewhere to hide her.

One day she came in from the garden utterly distraught. A few minutes earlier – and she pointed to the spot – father and daughter had appeared to her, doing nothing, but simply looking at her.

For several months she stayed in her room in a kind of stupor. Félicité scolded her gently, telling her that she must take care of herself for her son's sake, and also in remembrance of 'her'.

'Her?' repeated Mme Aubain, as if she were waking from a sleep. 'Oh, yes, of course! You don't forget her, do you!' This was an allusion to the cemetery, where she herself was strictly forbidden to go.

Félicité went there every day. She would set out on the stroke of four, going past the houses, up the hill, and through the gate, until she came to Virginie's grave. There was a little column of pink marble with a tablet at its base, and a tiny garden enclosed by chains. The beds were hidden under a carpet of flowers. She watered their leaves and changed the sand, going down on her knees to fork the ground thoroughly. The result was that when Mme Aubain was able to come here, she experienced a feeling of relief, a kind of consolation.

Then the years slipped by, each one like the last, with nothing to vary the rhythm of the great festivals: Easter, the Assumption, All Saints' Day. Domestic events marked dates that later served as points of reference. Thus in 1825 a couple of glaziers whitewashed the hall; in 1827 a piece of the roof fell into the courtyard and nearly killed a man; and in the summer of 1828 it was Madame's turn to provide the bread for consecration. About this time Bourais went away in a mysterious fashion; and one by one the old acquaintances disappeared: Guyot, Liébard, Mme Lechaptois, Robelin, and Uncle Grémanville, who had been paralysed for a long time.

One night the driver of the mail-coach brought Pont-l'Évêque news of the July Revolution. A few days later a new sub-prefect was appointed. This was the Baron de Larsonnière, who had been a consul in America, and who brought with him, besides his wife, his sister-in-law and three young ladies who were almost grown-up. They were to be seen on their lawn, dressed in loose-fitting smocks; and they had a Negro servant and a parrot. They paid a call on Mme Aubain, who made a point of returning it. As soon as Félicité saw them coming, she would run and tell her mistress. But only one thing could really awaken her interest, and that was her son's letters.

He seemed to be incapable of following any career and spent all his time in taverns. She paid his debts, but he contracted new ones, and the sighs Mme Aubain heaved as she knitted by the window reached Félicité at her spinning-wheel in the kitchen.

The two women used to walk up and down together beside the espalier, forever talking of Virginie and debating whether such and such a thing would have appealed to her, or what she would have said on such and such an occasion.

All her little belongings were in a cupboard in the children's bedroom. Mme Aubain went through them as seldom as possible. One summer day she resigned herself to doing so, and the moths were sent fluttering out of the cupboard.

Virginie's frocks hung in a row underneath a shelf containing three dolls, a few hoops, a set of toy furniture, and the wash-basin she had used. Besides the frocks, they took out her petticoats, her stockings and her handkerchiefs, and spread them out on the two beds before folding them up again. The sunlight streamed in on these pathetic objects, bringing out the stains and showing up the creases made by the child's movements. The air was warm, the sky was blue, a blackbird was singing, and everything seemed to be utterly at peace.

They found a little chestnut-coloured hat, made of plush with a long nap; but the moths had ruined it. Félicité asked if she might have it. The two women looked at each other and their eyes filled with tears. Then the mistress opened her arms, the maid threw herself into them, and they clasped each other in a warm embrace, satisfying their grief in a kiss which made them equal.

It was the first time that such a thing had happened, for Mme Aubain was not of a demonstrative nature. Félicité was as grateful as if she had received a great favour, and henceforth loved her mistress with dog-like devotion and religious veneration.

Her heart grew softer as time went by.

When she heard the drums of a regiment coming down the street she stood at the door with a jug of cider and offered the soldiers a drink. She looked after the people who went down with cholera. She watched over the Polish refugees, and one of them actually expressed a desire to marry her. But they fell out, for when she came back from the Angelus one morning, she found that he had got into her kitchen and was calmly eating an oil-and-vinegar salad.

After the Poles it was Père Colmiche, an old man who was said to have committed fearful atrocities in '93. He lived by the river in a ruined pig-sty. The boys of the town used to peer at him through the cracks in the walls, and threw pebbles at him which landed on the litter where he lay, constantly shaken by fits of coughing. His hair was extremely long, his eyelids inflamed, and on one arm there was a swelling bigger than his head. Félicité brought him some linen, tried to clean out his filthy hovel, and even wondered if she could install him in the wash-house without annoying Madame. When the tumour had burst, she changed his dressings every day, brought him some cake now and then, and put him out in the sun on a truss of hay. The poor old fellow would thank her in a faint whisper, slavering and trembling all the while, fearful of losing her and stretching his hands out as soon as he saw her moving away.

He died, and she had a Mass said for the repose of his soul.

That same day a great piece of good fortune came her way. Just as she was serving dinner, Mme de Larsonnière's Negro appeared carrying the parrot in its cage, complete with perch, chain, and padlock. The Baroness had written a note informing Mme Aubain that her husband had been promoted to a

Prefecture and they were leaving that evening; she begged her to accept the parrot as a keepsake and a token of her regard.

This bird had engrossed Félicité's thoughts for a long time, for it came from America, and that word reminded her of Victor. So she had asked the Negro all about it, and once she had even gone so far as to say:

'How pleased Madame would be if it were hers!'

The Negro had repeated this remark to his mistress, who, unable to take the parrot with her, was glad to get rid of it in this way.

4

His name was Loulou. His body was green, the tips of his wings were pink, his poll blue, and his breast golden.

Unfortunately he had a tiresome mania for biting his perch, and also used to pull his feathers out, scatter his droppings everywhere, and upset his bath water. He annoyed Mme Aubain, and so she gave him to Félicité for good.

Félicité started training him, and soon he could say: 'Nice boy! Your servant, sir! Hail, Mary!' He was put near the door, and several people who spoke to him said how strange it was that he did not answer to the name of Jacquot, as all parrots were called Jacquot. They likened him to a turkey or a block of wood, and every sneer cut Félicité to the quick. How odd, she thought, that Loulou should be so stubborn, refusing to talk whenever anyone looked at him!

For all that, he liked having people around him, because on Sundays, while the Rochefeuille sisters, M. Houppeville and some new friends – the apothecary Onfroy, M. Varin, and Captain Mathieu – were having their game of cards, he would beat on the window-panes with his wings and make such a din that it was impossible to hear oneself speak.

Bourais's face obviously struck him as terribly funny, for as soon as he saw it he was seized with uncontrollable laughter. His shrieks rang round the courtyard, the echo repeated them, and the neighbours came to their windows and started laughing too. To avoid being seen by the bird, M. Bourais used to creep along by the wall, hiding his face behind his hat, until he got to the river, and then come into the house from the garden. The looks he gave the parrot were far from tender.

Loulou had once been cuffed by the butcher's boy for poking his head into his basket; and since then he was always trying to give him a nip through his shirt. Fabu threatened to wring his neck, although he was not a cruel fellow, in spite of his tattooed arms and bushy whiskers. On the contrary, he rather liked the parrot, so much so indeed that in a spirit of jovial camaraderie he tried to teach him a few swear-words. Félicité, alarmed at this development, put the bird in the kitchen. His little chain was removed and he was allowed to wander all over the house.

Coming downstairs, he used to rest the curved part of his beak on each step and then raise first his right foot, then his left; and Félicité was afraid that this sort of gymnastic performance would make him giddy. He fell ill and could neither talk nor eat for there was a swelling under his tongue such as hens sometimes have. She cured him by pulling this pellicule out with her finger-nails. One day M. Paul was silly enough to blow the smoke of his cigar at him; another time Mme Lormeau started teasing him with the end of her parasol, and he caught hold of the ferrule with his beak. Finally he got lost.

Félicité had put him down on the grass in the fresh air, and left him there for a minute. When she came back, the parrot had gone. First of all she looked for him in the bushes, by the river and on the rooftops, paying no attention to her mistress's shouts of: 'Be careful, now! You must be mad!' Next she went over all the gardens in Pont-l'Évêque, stopping passersby and asking them: 'You don't happen to have seen my parrot by any chance?' Those who did not know him already were given a description of the bird. Suddenly she thought she could make out something green flying about behind the mills at the foot of the hill. But up on the hill there was nothing to be seen. A pedlar told her that he had come upon the parrot a short time before in Mère Simon's shop at Saint-Melaine. She ran all the way there, but no one knew what she was talking about. Finally she came back home, worn out, her shoes falling to pieces, and death in her heart. She was sitting beside Madame on the garden-seat and telling her what she had been doing, when she felt something light drop on her shoulder. It was Loulou! What he had been up to, no one could discover: perhaps he had just gone for a little walk round the town.

Félicité was slow to recover from this fright, and indeed never really got over it.

As the result of a chill she had an attack of quinsy, and soon after that her ears were affected. Three years later she was deaf, and she spoke at the top of her voice, even in church. Although her sins could have been proclaimed over the length and breadth of the diocese without dishonour to her or offence to others, M. le Curé thought it advisable to hear her confession in the sacristy.

Imaginary buzzings in the head added to her troubles. Often her mistress would say: 'Heavens, how stupid you are!' and she would reply: 'Yes, Madame', at the same time looking all around her for something.

The little circle of her ideas grew narrower and narrower, and the pealing of bells and the lowing of cattle went out of her life. Every living thing moved about in a ghostly silence. Only one sound reached her ears now, and that was the voice of the parrot.

As if to amuse her, he would reproduce the click-clack of the turn-spit, the shrill call of a man selling fish, and the noise of the saw at the joiner's across the way; and when the bell rang he would imitate Mme Aubain's 'Félicité! The door, the door!'

They held conversations with each other, he repeating *ad nauseam* the three phrases in his repertory, she replying with words which were just as disconnected but which came from the heart. In her isolation, Loulou was almost a son or a lover to her. He used to climb up her fingers, peck at her lips, and hang on to her shawl; and as she bent over him, wagging her head from side to side as nurses do, the great wings of her bonnet and the wings of the bird quivered in unison.

When clouds banked up in the sky and there was a rumbling of thunder, he would utter piercing cries, no doubt remembering the sudden downpours in his native forests. The sound of the rain falling roused him to frenzy. He would flap excitedly around, shoot up to the ceiling, knocking everything over, and fly out of the window to splash about in the garden. But he would soon come back to perch on one of the firedogs, hopping about to dry his feathers and showing tail and beak in turn.

One morning in the terrible winter of 1837, when she had put him in front of the fire because of the cold she found him dead in the middle of his cage, hanging head down with his claws caught in the bars. He had probably died of a stroke, but she thought he had been poisoned with parsley, and despite the absence of any proof, her suspicions fell on Fabu.

She wept so much that her mistress said to her: 'Why don't you have him stuffed?'

Félicité asked the chemist's advice, remembering that he had always been kind to the parrot. He wrote to Le Havre, and a man called Fellacher agreed to do the job. As parcels sometimes went astray on the mail-coach, she decided to take the parrot as far as Honfleur herself.

On either side of the road stretched an endless succession of apple-trees, all stripped of their leaves, and there was ice in the ditches. Dogs were barking around the farms; and Félicité, with her hands tucked under her mantlet, her little black sabots and her basket, walked briskly along the middle of the road.

She crossed the forest, passed Le Haut-Chêne, and got as far as Saint-Gatien.

Behind her, in a cloud of dust, and gathering speed as the horses galloped downhill, a mail-coach swept along like a whirlwind. When he saw this woman making no attempt to get out of the way, the driver poked his head out above the hood, and he and the postilion shouted at her. His four horses could not be held in and galloped faster, the two leaders touching her as they went by. With a jerk of the reins the driver threw them to one side, and then, in a fury, he raised his long whip and gave her such a lash, from head to waist, that she fell flat on her back.

The first thing she did on regaining consciousness was to open her basket. Fortunately nothing had happened to Loulou. She felt her right cheek burning, and when she touched it her hand turned red; it was bleeding.

She sat down on a heap of stones and dabbed her face with her handkerchief. Then she ate a crust of bread which she had taken the precaution of putting in her basket, and tried to forget her wound by looking at the bird.

As she reached the top of the hill at Ecquemauville, she saw the lights of Honfleur twinkling in the darkness like a host of stars, and the shadowy expanse of the sea beyond. Then a sudden feeling of faintness made her stop; and the misery of her childhood, the disappointment of her first love, the departure of her nephew, and the death of Virginie all came back to her at once like the waves of a rising tide, and, welling up in her throat, choked her.

When she got to the boat she insisted on speaking to the

captain, and without telling him what was in her parcel, asked him to take good care of it.

Fellacher kept the parrot a long time. Every week he promised it for the next; after six months he announced that a box had been sent off, and nothing more was heard of it. It looked as though Loulou would never come back, and Félicité told herself: 'They've stolen him for sure!'

At last he arrived – looking quite magnificent, perched on a branch screwed into a mahogany base, one foot in the air, his head cocked to one side, and biting a nut which the taxidermist, out of a love of the grandiose, had gilded.

Félicité shut him up in her room.

This place, to which few people were ever admitted, contained such a quantity of religious bric-à-brac and miscellaneous oddments that it looked like a cross between a chapel and a bazaar.

A big wardrobe prevented the door from opening properly. Opposite the window that overlooked the garden was a little round one looking on to the courtyard. There was a table beside the bed, with a water-jug, a couple of combs, and a block of blue soap in a chipped plate. On the walls there were rosaries, medals, several pictures of the Virgin, and a holy-water stoup made out of a coconut. On the chest of drawers, which was draped with a cloth just like an altar, was the shell box Victor had given her, and also a watering-can and a ball, some copy-books, the illustrated geography book, and a pair of ankle-boots. And on the nail supporting the looking-glass, fastened by its ribbons, hung the little plush hat.

Félicité carried this form of veneration to such lengths that she even kept one of Monsieur's frock-coats. All the old rubbish Mme Aubain had no more use for, she carried off to her room. That was how there came to be artificial flowers along the edge of the chest of drawers, and a portrait of the Comte d'Artois in the window-recess.

With the aid of a wall-bracket, Loulou was installed on a chimney-breast that jutted out into the room. Every morning when she awoke, she saw him in the light of the dawn, and then she remembered the old days, and the smallest details of insignificant actions, not in sorrow but in absolute tranquillity.

Having no intercourse with anyone, she lived in the torpid state of a sleep-walker. The Corpus Christi processions roused her from this condition, for she would go round the neighbours collecting candlesticks and mats to decorate the altar of repose which they used to set up in the street.

In church she was forever gazing at the Holy Ghost, and one day she noticed that it had something of the parrot about it. This resemblance struck her as even more obvious in a colour-print depicting the baptism of Our Lord. With its red wings and its emerald-green body, it was the very image of Loulou.

She bought the print and hung it in the place of the Comte d'Artois, so that she could include them both in a single glance. They were linked together in her mind, the parrot being sanctified by this connexion with the Holy Ghost, which itself acquired new life and meaning in her eyes. God the Father could not have chosen a dove as a means of expressing Himself, since doves cannot talk, but rather one of Loulou's ancestors. And although Félicité used to say her prayers with her eyes on the picture, from time to time she would turn slightly towards the bird.

She wanted to join the Children of Mary, but Mme Aubain dissuaded her from doing so.

An important event now loomed up – Paul's wedding.

After starting as a lawyer's clerk, he had been in business, in the Customs, and in Inland Revenue, and had even begun trying to get into the Department of Woods and Forests, when, at the age of thirty-six, by some heaven-sent inspiration, he suddenly discovered his real vocation – in the Wills and Probate Department. There he proved so capable that one of the auditors had offered him his daughter in marriage and promised to use his influence on his behalf.

Paul, grown serious-minded, brought her to see his mother. She criticized the way things were done at Pont-l'Évêque, put on airs, and hurt Félicité's feelings. Mme Aubain was relieved to see her go.

The following week came news of M. Bourais's death in an inn in Lower Brittany. Rumours that he had committed suicide were confirmed, and doubts arose as to his honesty. Mme Aubain went over her accounts and was soon conversant with the full catalogue of his misdeeds – embezzlement of interest, secret sales of timber, forged receipts, etc. Besides all this, he was the father of an illegitimate child, and had had 'relations with a person at Dozulé'.

These infamies upset Mme Aubain greatly. In March 1853 she was afflicted with a pain in the chest; her tongue seemed to be covered with a film; leeches failed to make her breathing any easier; and on the ninth evening of her illness she died. She had just reached the age of seventy-two.

She was thought to be younger because of her brown hair, worn in bandeaux round her pale, pock-marked face. There were few friends to mourn her, for she had a haughty manner which put people off. Yet Félicité wept for her as servants rarely weep for their masters. That Madame should die before her upset her ideas, seemed to be contrary to the order of things, monstrous and unthinkable.

Ten days later – the time it took to travel hot-foot from Besançon – the heirs arrived. The daughter-in-law ransacked every drawer, picked out some pieces of furniture and sold the rest; and then back they went to the Wills and Probate Department.

Madame's arm-chair, her pedestal table, her foot-warmer, and the eight chairs had all gone. Yellow squares in the centre of the wall-panels showed where the pictures had hung. They had carried off the two cots with their mattresses, and no trace remained in the cupboard of all Virginie's things. Félicité climbed the stairs to her room, numbed with sadness.

The next day there was a notice on the door, and the apothecary shouted in her ear that the house was up for sale.

She swayed on her feet, and was obliged to sit down.

What distressed her most of all was the idea of leaving her room, which was so suitable for poor Loulou. Fixing an anguished look on him as she appealed to the Holy Ghost, she contracted the idolatrous habit of kneeling in front of the parrot to say her prayers. Sometimes the sun, as it came through the little window, caught his glass eye, so that it shot out a great luminous ray which sent her into ecstasies.

She had a pension of three hundred and eighty francs a year which her mistress had left her. The garden kept her in vegetables. As for clothes, she had enough to last her till the end of her days, and she saved on lighting by going to bed as soon as darkness fell.

She went out as little as possible, to avoid the second-hand dealer's shop, where some of the old furniture was on display. Ever since her fit of giddiness, she had been dragging one leg; and as her strength was failing, Mère Simon, whose grocery business had come to grief, came in every morning to chop wood and pump water for her.

Her eyes grew weaker. The shutters were not opened any more. Years went by, and nobody rented the house and nobody bought it.

For fear of being evicted, Félicité never asked for any repairs to be done. The laths in the roof rotted, and all through one winter her bolster was wet. After Easter she began spitting blood.

When this happened Mère Simon called in a doctor. Félicité wanted to know what was the matter with her, but she was so deaf that only one word reached her: 'Pneumonia.' It was a word she knew, and she answered gently: 'Ah! like Madame', thinking it natural that she should follow in her mistress's footsteps.

The time to set up the altars of repose was drawing near.

The first altar was always at the foot of the hill, the second in front of the post office, the third about half-way up the street. There was some argument as to the siting of this one, and finally the women of the parish picked on Mme Aubain's courtyard.

The fever and the tightness of the chest grew worse. Félicité fretted over not doing anything for the altar. If only she could have put something on it! Then she thought of the parrot. The neighbours protested that it would not be seemly, but the curé gave his permission, and this made her so happy that she begged him to accept Loulou, the only thing of value she possessed, when she died.

From Tuesday to Saturday, the eve of Corpus Christi, she coughed more and more frequently. In the evening her face looked pinched and drawn, her lips stuck to her gums, and she started vomiting. At dawn the next day, feeling very low, she sent for a priest.

Three good women stood by her while she was given extreme unction. Then she said that she had to speak to Fabu.

He arrived in his Sunday best, very ill at ease in this funereal atmosphere.

'Forgive me,' she said, making an effort to stretch out her arm. 'I thought it was you who had killed him.'

What could she mean by such nonsense? To think that she had suspected a man like him of murder! He got very indignant and was obviously going to make a scene.

'Can't you see', they said, 'that she isn't in her right mind any more?'

From time to time Félicité would start talking to shadows. The women went away. Mère Simon had her lunch.

A little later she picked Loulou up and held him out to Félicité, saying:

'Come now, say good-bye to him.'

Although the parrot was not a corpse, the worms were eating him up. One of his wings was broken, and the stuffing was coming out of his stomach. But she was blind by now, and she kissed him on the forehead and pressed him against her cheek. Mère Simon took him away from her to put him on the altar.

5

THE scents of summer came up from the meadows; there was a buzzing of flies; the sun was glittering in the river and warming the slates of the roof. Mère Simon had come back into the room and was gently nodding off to sleep.

The noise of church bells woke her up; the congregation was coming out from vespers. Félicité's delirium abated. Thinking of the procession, she could see it as clearly as if she had been following it.

All the school-children, the choristers, and the firemen were walking along the pavements, while advancing up the middle of the street came the church officer armed with his halberd, the beadle carrying a great cross, the schoolmaster keeping an eye on the boys, and the nun fussing over her little girls – three of the prettiest, looking like curly-headed angels, were throwing rose-petals into the air. Then came the deacon, with both arms outstretched, conducting the band, and a couple of censer-bearers who turned round at every step to face the Holy Sacrament, which the curé, wearing his splendid chasuble, was carrying under a canopy of poppy-red velvet held aloft by four churchwardens. A crowd of people surged along behind, between the white cloths covering the walls of the houses, and eventually they got to the bottom of the hill.

A cold sweat moistened Félicité's temples. Mère Simon sponged it up with a cloth, telling herself that one day she would have to go the same way.

The hum of the crowd increased in volume, was very loud for a moment, then faded away.

A fusillade shook the window-panes. It was the postilions saluting the monstrance. Félicité rolled her eyes and said as loud as she could: 'Is he all right?' – worrying about the parrot.

She entered into her death-agony. Her breath, coming ever faster, with a rattling sound, made her sides heave. Bubbles of froth appeared at the corners of her mouth, and her whole body trembled.

Soon the booming of the ophicleides, the clear voices of the children, and the deep voices of the men could be heard near at hand. Now and then everything was quiet, and the tramping of feet, deadened by a carpet of flowers, sounded like a flock moving across pasture-land.

The clergy appeared in the courtyard. Mère Simon climbed on to a chair to reach the little round window, from which she had a full view of the altar below.

It was hung with green garlands and adorned with a flounce in English needle-point lace. In the middle was a little frame containing some relics, there were two orange-trees at the corners, and all the way along stood silver candlesticks and china vases holding sunflowers, lilies, peonies, foxgloves, and bunches of hydrangea. This pyramid of bright colours stretched from the first floor right down to the carpet which was spread out over the pavement. Some rare objects caught the eye: a silver-gilt sugar-basin wreathed in violets, some pendants of Alençon gems gleaming on a bed of moss, and two Chinese screens with landscape decorations. Loulou, hidden under roses, showed nothing but his blue poll, which looked like a plaque of lapis lazuli.

The churchwardens, the choristers, and the children lined up along the three sides of the courtyard. The priest went slowly up the steps and placed his great shining gold sun on the lace altar-cloth. Everyone knelt down. There was a deep silence. And the censers, swinging at full tilt, slid up and down their chains.

A blue cloud of incense was wafted up into Félicité's room. She opened her nostrils wide and breathed it in with a mystical, sensuous fervour. Then she closed her eyes. Her lips smiled. Her heart-beats grew slower and slower, each a little fainter and gentler, like a fountain running dry, an echo fading away. And as she breathed her last, she thought she could see, in the opening heavens, a gigantic parrot hovering above her head.

The Legend of St Julian Hospitator

Julian's father and mother lived in a castle in the middle of a forest, on the slope of a hill.

The four towers at its corners had pointed roofs covered with lead scales, and the base of the walls rested on blocks of solid rock which fell steeply to the bottom of the moat.

The pavement of the courtyard was as clean as the flag-stones of a church. Long gutter-spouts, shaped like dragons hanging head-down, spat all the rain-water into a cistern; and on every window-sill of every storey a basil or a heliotrope flowered in a painted earthenware pot.

Inside a second enclosure, made with stakes, there was first an orchard, then a garden plot in which flowers had been arranged to form figures, after that a pergola for taking the air, and finally an alley where the pages could play mall. On the other side were the kennels, the stables, the bakehouse, the press-house, and the barns. All round this there wound a strip of green grazing-ground, itself enclosed by a stout thorn-hedge.

Peace had prevailed for so long that the portcullis was not lowered any more, the moat was full of grass, swallows nested in the look-out slits, and the archer who patrolled the battlements all day retired to his watch-tower when the sun grew too hot and dozed off like a monk.

Inside the castle the ironwork shone brightly everywhere; tapestries lined the walls to keep out the cold; and the cup-boards were crammed with linen, the cellars piled high with tuns of wine, and the oak coffers creaking under the weight of money-bags.

In the armoury, between military standards and wild beasts'

heads, were to be seen weapons of every age and every nation, from Amalekite slings and Garamantian javelins to Saracen brackmards and Norman coats of mail.

The master-spit in the kitchen could roast an ox. The chapel was as magnificent as a king's oratory. There was even a bath-house of the Roman type tucked away somewhere, but the noble lord made no use of it as he held it to be a heathen institution.

Always wrapped in a mantle of fox pelts, he would stride about his castle, dispensing justice to his vassals and settling his neighbours' quarrels. In winter he watched the snowflakes falling or had stories read to him. When the first fine days came, he rode out on his mule along the by-paths, beside the green corn-fields, talking with the peasants and giving them advice.

After many adventures, he had taken a maiden of noble birth as his wife. She was very fair of skin, and somewhat proud and solemn. The horns of her coif brushed against the lintels of the doors; the train of her cloth dress trailed three paces behind her. Her household was as well-regulated as a monastery. Every morning she gave her serving-women their instructions, inspected the preserves and ointments, span on her distaff, or embroidered an altar-cloth. In answer to her prayers a son was born to her.

Then there was great merry-making, with a torchlight banquet which lasted three days and four nights, to the sound of harps, with green branches strewn on the flagstones. The rarest spices were eaten at this meal, and fowls as fat as sheep. To amuse the guests, a dwarf appeared out of a pie; and as more people kept arriving and there were not enough bowls to go round, they were obliged to drink out of horns and helmets.

The young mother took no part in these festivities, but remained quietly in bed. One night she awoke and, in the moonlight which shone through her window, she saw what appeared to be a shadow moving. It was an old man in a homespun robe, with a rosary at his side and a wallet across his shoulder, looking just like a hermit. He came up to her bed and without opening his lips said:

'Rejoice, mother, for your son shall be a saint!'

She was about to cry out but, gliding along the moonbeam, he rose gently into the air and disappeared. The songs of the guests burst forth louder than ever. She heard the voices of angels, and her head fell back upon the pillows, over which there hung a martyr's bone set in a frame of garnets.

The next day all the servants were questioned, and all denied having seen the hermit. Dream or reality, this was obviously a message from heaven, but she was careful to say nothing about it, for fear that she should be accused of pride.

At dawn the guests departed. Julian's father was standing outside the postern-gate, where he had just taken leave of the last of them, when suddenly a beggar rose up before him out of the mist. The man was a gipsy with a plaited beard, silver bracelets on his arms, and blazing eyes. As though inspired, he stammered out these disconnected words:

'Ah! Ah! Your son! Much bloodshed! Much glory! Always fortunate! An emperor's family!'

And, bending down to pick up his alms, he disappeared in the grass and vanished from sight.

The noble lord looked around and called out with all his might. There was no one there; only the whistling wind, and the morning mists drifting away.

He attributed this vision to weariness from having too little sleep. 'If I mention it, they will only laugh at me,' he thought. But the glorious destiny promised to his son dazzled him, although the promise was not clear and he was not even certain that he had heard it.

He and his wife kept their secrets from each other. But they both cherished their child equally and, respecting him as one marked out by God, lavished infinite care upon him. His cradle was padded with the finest down; a lamp in the shape of a dove burned continually above it; three nurses rocked him to sleep. Wrapped in his swaddling clothes, with his pink face and blue eyes, his mantle of brocade and his bonnet loaded with pearls, he looked like an Infant Jesus. He cut all his teeth without crying once.

When he was seven his mother taught him to sing, and his father, to give him courage, hoisted him on to a big horse. The boy smiled with pleasure and soon knew all about chargers.

A very learned old monk taught him Holy Scripture, the Arabic numerals, the Latin letters, and the art of painting miniatures on vellum. They used to work together high up in a turret where there was no noise to disturb them. When a lesson was over they would go down into the garden, where they studied the flowers as they walked slowly up and down.

Sometimes a string of pack-animals was seen making its way along the valley below, led by a man on foot in Eastern garb. The lord of the castle, recognizing the man for a merchant, would send a servant out to him, and the stranger would trustfully turn aside from his path. Ushered into the parlour, he would bring out of his chests pieces of velvet and silk, jewels and spices, and curious things of unknown use; and eventually he would take his leave, having made a handsome profit and suffered no violence.

At other times a band of pilgrims would come knocking at the gate. Their wet clothes would steam in front of the fire, and when they had eaten their fill they would tell stories of their travels – of voyages across foaming seas, marches across burning sands, the cruelty of the heathen, the Syrian caves, the Manger, and the Sepulchre. And then they would give the young lord scallop-shells from their cloaks.

Often the lord of the castle gave a feast to his old comrades in arms. As they drank together they talked about the battles they had fought and the fortresses they had stormed, recalling fabulous wounds and the thunderous din of the engines of war. Julian gave cries of delight as he listened to them, and then his father felt sure that one day he would be a conqueror. But every evening, as he came out from the Angelus and passed between rows of poor people bowing before him, he would dip into his purse with such modesty and nobility that his mother was certain that she would live to see him an arch-bishop.

His place in the chapel was beside his parents, and however long the office might be, he remained kneeling at his stool, his hat on the floor and his hands clasped in prayer.

One day, during Mass, he looked up and noticed a little white mouse coming out of a hole in the wall. It trotted along the first of the altar steps, and after turning right and left two or three times, ran back the way it had come. The following Sunday he was disturbed by the thought that he might see it again. It did come back, and every Sunday he watched for it with growing irritation, until at last he was seized with hatred for the creature and decided to get rid of it.

So, after closing the door and sprinkling some cake crumbs on the altar steps, he stationed himself in front of the hole with a stick in his hand.

After a long time a pink nose appeared, followed by the rest of the mouse. He gave it a light tap, and was astonished to see the little body lie there without moving. A drop of blood showed on the flagstone. He quickly wiped it off with his sleeve, threw the mouse away outside, and said nothing about it to anyone.

All sorts of birds used to peck at the seeds in the garden. He hit upon the idea of shooting peas at them through a hollow reed, and whenever he heard a twittering in the trees, he crept up quietly, raised his pipe, and puffed out his cheeks. The little creatures rained down on his shoulders in such abundance that he could not help laughing, he was so pleased at his cleverness.

One morning, as he was coming back along the battlements, he saw a fat pigeon preening itself in the sunshine on the crest of the wall. He stopped to look at it, and since there was a breach in this part of the wall his fingers happened on a lump of stone. He swung his arm, the stone hit the bird, and it dropped like a plummet into the moat.

He dashed down after it, tearing his skin in the undergrowth and ferreting around everywhere, as nimble as a puppy.

The pigeon, its wings broken and its body quivering, was caught in the branches of a privet.

Its stubborn refusal to die infuriated the child. He set about wringing its neck, and its convulsions made his heart beat wildly, filling him with a savage, passionate delight. When it finally went stiff in his hands he felt he was going to faint.

That evening, during supper, his father declared that he was old enough to begin learning the art of venery, and he went to look for an old copy-book of his which contained, in the form of questions and answers, all there was to be known about the chase. In this book a master explained to his pupil the art of training hounds, taming falcons, and setting snares; how to recognize a stag by its droppings, a fox by its tracks, a wolf by the scratches it left on the ground; the best way of distinguishing their spoor, how to start them, where their lairs were likely to be found, which were the most favourable winds, and what were the calls and rules of the kill.

As soon as Julian could recite all these things by heart, his father got together a pack of hounds for him. It included twenty-four Barbary greyhounds, swifter than gazelles but liable to bolt, and seventeen pairs of Breton dogs, with russet coats and white markings, sure in their judgement, strong in the chest, and mighty bayers. For the attack on the boar and other dangerous situations, there were forty griffon terriers, as haggy as bears. Then there were some flame-coloured Tartary mastiffs, almost as big as donkeys, with broad backs and long legs, which were intended for hunting the wild ox. The black coats of the spaniels shone like satin; the yelping of the talbots rivalled the chanting of the beagles. In a yard by themselves, growling, shaking their chains, and rolling their eyes, were eight alans, formidable brutes which would fly at a horseman's belly and were not afraid of lions.

All these hounds were fed on wheaten bread, drank out of stone troughs, and bore high-sounding names.

The falcons were perhaps even more remarkable than the hounds, for the noble lord had obtained, at great expense, tercelets from the Caucasus, sakers from Babylon, gerfalcons from Germany, and peregrine falcons captured on cliffs beside icy seas in far-off lands. They were housed in a thatched shed, chained to their perch according to size, with a strip of turf in front of them on which they were placed from time to time to loosen their limbs.

Bag-nets, hooks, wolf-traps, and all kinds of other devices were put together.

Often they took setters out into the country, and it was never long before they came to a point. Then the prickers, creeping slowly forward, carefully spread a huge net over their motionless bodies. At a word of command they started barking, and quail flew up into the net. The ladies of the neighbourhood, invited to the hunt with their husbands, their children, and their handmaids, all threw themselves upon the birds and caught them easily.

At other times drums were beaten to start hares, foxes fell into pits, or the spring of a trap uncoiled and caught a wolf by its paw.

But Julian despised these facile contrivances and preferred to go hunting on his own, with his horse and his falcon. This was nearly always a great Scythian tartar as white as snow. Its leather hood was topped with a plume, golden bells jangled on its blue feet, and it stood fast on its master's arm while the horse galloped along and the plains unfolded before them. Slipping its jesses, Julian would suddenly let it go; the fearless bird would soar into the air as straight as an arrow; and soon two specks of unequal size would be seen circling, meeting, and disappearing in the blue skies above. Then the falcon would come down, tearing some bird to pieces, and return to settle on the gauntlet with its wings quivering.

In this way Julian flew herons, kites, crows, and vultures.

He loved to sound his horn and follow his hounds as they coursed along the hill slopes, jumped the streams, and climbed up to the woods again; and when the stag began to groan under their bites, he would kill it quickly and then watch with delight as the mastiffs frantically devoured the carcass, chopped in pieces on its reeking hide.

On misty days he plunged deep into a marsh to lie in wait for geese, otters, and young wild-duck.

At dawn every day three squires used to wait for him at the foot of the steps; and although the old monk, leaning out of his window, might beckon him back, he never turned round. He went off in the heat of the sun, in pouring rain, or at the height of a storm, drinking spring-water from the hollow of his hand, eating wild apples as he jogged along, and resting under an oak if he was tired; and he came home in the middle of the night, covered with blood and mud, with thorns in his hair and the smell of wild beasts all about him. He grew to resemble them. When his mother kissed him, he submitted coldly to her embrace and seemed to be pondering over weighty matters.

He killed bears with a knife, bulls with an axe, and boars with a spear; and once he even made do with a stick, the only weapon he had, to defend himself against some wolves which were gnawing the corpses at the foot of a gibbet.

One winter morning he set off before dawn, well equipped, with a cross-bow on his shoulder and a quiver of arrows at his saddle-bow.

His Danish jennet, followed by a pair of basset hounds, trotted along at a steady pace, making the ground ring with the sound of its hoofs. Drops of rime clung to his cloak and a stiff breeze was blowing. One side of the horizon cleared, and in the pale morning twilight he noticed some rabbits hopping about outside their burrows. The two basset hounds promptly rushed at them and swiftly broke a few backs.

Soon afterwards he entered a forest. A wood-grouse, numbed by the cold, was asleep on the end of a branch with its head under its wing. With a backward sweep of his sword, Julian lopped its feet off, and went on his way without stopping to pick it up.

Three hours later he found himself on the peak of a mountain so high that the sky seemed almost black. Sloping away in front of him was a rock like a long wall which hung over an abyss, and at the far end two wild goats were looking into the chasm beneath. Not having any arrows with him, for he had left his horse further back, he decided to go down to where they were. Bent nearly double and barefooted, he finally reached the first of the two goats and plunged a dagger between its ribs. The other animal, seized with panic, leapt into the void. Julian sprang forward to stab it, his right foot slipped, and he fell on top of the first goat's carcass, with his arms outspread and his head hanging over the abyss.

Going down into the plain again, he followed a line of willows growing alongside a river. From time to time cranes, flying very low, passed over his head. He struck them down with his whip and never missed his aim.

Meanwhile the milder air had melted the hoar frost, trails of mist were swirling around and at last the sun appeared. In the distance Julian saw a gleaming lake, so still that it looked like lead. In the middle of it was an animal he did not recognize, a black-nosed beaver. In spite of the distance an arrow killed it and he was annoyed at not being able to carry off its skin.

Then he went along an avenue of great trees, whose top formed a kind of triumphal arch leading into a forest. A roe bounded out of a covert, a buck appeared at a cross-way, a badger came out of a hole, and a peacock spread its tail on the grass. And when he had killed them all, more roes came forward, more bucks, more badgers, more peacocks, together with blackbirds, jays, polecats, foxes, hedgehogs, and lynxes - an endless succession of birds and beasts growing more numerous at every step. They circled round him, all trembling and gazing at him with gentle, supplicating eyes. But Julian did not tire of killing, first drawing his cross-bow, then unsheathing his sword and after that thrusting with his knife. He had no thought or recollection of anything at all. Only the fact of his being alive told him that he had been hunting for an indefinite time in some indeterminate place, for everything happened with dreamlike ease.

An extraordinary sight brought him to a halt. Before him lay a valley shaped like an amphitheatre and filled with stags. They were crowded close together, warming each other with their breath, which he could see steaming in the mist.

For a few minutes the prospect of such carnage as this left him breathless with delight. Then he dismounted, rolled up his sleeves, and began shooting.

As the first arrow whistled through the air, all the stags turned their heads at once. Gaps appeared in their midst, plaintive cries arose, and a great tremor went through the herd.

The lip of the valley was too high to climb, and they bounded about in the enclosure, looking for a means of escape. Julian went on taking aim and shooting, and his arrows fell like shafts of rain in a heavy storm. The maddened stags fought, reared up in the air, and climbed on each other's backs, their bodies and tangled antlers making a broad mound which kept shifting and crumbling.

At last they died, stretched out on the sand, their nostrils foaming, their entrails gushing out, and the heaving of their bellies gradually subsiding. Then all was still.

Night was drawing on, and behind the forest, through the spaces in the branches, the sky showed red like a sheet of blood.

Julian leant back against a tree, considering with wide-eyed wonderment the magnitude of the slaughter, unable to understand how he could have carried it out.

Then, on the far side of the valley, at the edge of the forest, he saw a stag with a doe and its fawn.

The stag was a huge black beast, a sixteen-pointer with a white beard. The doe, as light in colour as a dead leaf, was cropping the grass, while the dappled fawn, without impeding her movements, pulled at her dugs.

Once again the cross-bow twanged. The fawn was killed instantly. Then its mother, looking up at the sky, gave a deep, heart-rending, human cry. Julian, exasperated, stretched her on the ground with a shot full in the breast.

The great stag had seen him and bounded forward. Julian sent his last arrow at him. It struck him in the forehead and remained planted there.

The great stag did not seem to feel it. Striding over the dead bodies, it came steadily nearer, apparently bent on attacking and disembowelling him. Julian fell back in unspeakable terror. The huge beast stopped; and with blazing eyes, solemn as a patriarch or a judge, and to the accompaniment of a bell tolling in the distance, it said three times:

'Accursed, accursed, accursed! One day, cruel heart, you will kill your father and mother!'

The stag's knees gave way, its eyes gently closed, and it died.

Julian was dumbfounded, and then suddenly overwhelmed

with fatigue; disgust and a feeling of infinite sadness took hold of him. He wept for a long time, his face buried in his hands.

His horse was lost, his hounds had left him, and the solitude which surrounded him seemed pregnant with indefinable perils. Filled with fear, he set off across country, choosing a path at random, and found himself almost at once at the castle gate.

He could not sleep that night. By the flickering light of the hanging lamp he kept seeing the great black stag. He was obsessed by the animal's prophecy and tried to fight against it. 'No, no, no!' he told himself. 'I cannot possibly kill them!' Then he thought: 'But what if I wanted to?' And he was afraid that the Devil might inspire him with that desire.

For three whole months his anguished mother prayed by his bedside, and his father paced up and down the corridors groaning. He sent for the most famous doctors, who prescribed innumerable drugs. Julian's illness, they said, was caused by some noxious wind or some amorous desire. But the young man shook his head in answer to all the questions that were asked him.

His strength revived and he was taken for walks round the courtyard, the old monk and the noble lord each supporting him with an arm.

When he had completely recovered he stubbornly refused to go hunting.

His father, wanting to make him happy, made him a present of a great Saracen sword. It hung with other weapons at the top of a pillar, and a ladder was needed to reach it. Julian climbed up.

The sword was too heavy and slipped out of his grasp, falling so close to the noble lord that it cut his surcoat. Julian thought that he had killed his father, and fainted.

From then on he had a dread of weapons. The sight of a naked blade made him turn pale. This weakness caused his parents great distress, and at last the old monk ordered him in the name of God, of honour and his ancestors, to take up a nobleman's pursuits once more.

Every day the squires used to amuse themselves by practising with the javelin. Julian very soon excelled at this sport. He could throw his javelin into the neck of a bottle, break the pointers of a weather-vane, and hit the nails in a door at a hundred paces.

One summer evening, at the hour when mist makes things indistinct, he was standing under the pergola in the garden and saw at the far end two white wings fluttering along the top of the wall. He was sure that this was a stork, and he threw his javelin.

A piercing shriek rang out.

It was his mother, whose coif with its long flaps remained nailed to the wall.

Julian fled from the castle and never came back.

2

HE enlisted in a troop of soldiers of fortune which was passing by.

He came to know hunger and thirst, fever and vermin. He grew accustomed to the noise of battle and the sight of death. The wind tanned his skin; the wearing of armour toughened his limbs; and as he was strong, courageous, temperate, and intelligent, he was soon given command of a company.

At the start of a battle he would urge his men forward with a great flourish of his sword. With the aid of a knotted rope he would scale the walls of citadels by night, swinging to and fro in the gale, while flakes of Greek fire stuck to his cuirass and boiling resin and molten lead poured from the battlements. Often a falling stone shattered his buckler. Bridges overladen with men gave way under him. Swinging his mace, he disposed of fourteen horsemen. He defeated every challenger who entered the lists against him. Over a score of times he was left for dead.

Thanks to divine providence he always escaped with his life, for he protected churchmen, orphans, widows, and, most particularly, old men. When he saw an old man walking ahead of him, he would call out to him to show his face, as if he were afraid of killing him by mistake.

Runaway serfs, rebellious peasants, penniless bastards, and all manner of brave fellows flocked to his flag, and he formed an army of his own.

It grew. He became famous and sought after.

One after the other, he helped the Dauphin of France and the King of England, the Templars of Jerusalem and the Surena of the Parthians, the Negus of Abyssinia and the Emperor of Calicut. He fought against Scandinavians covered with fishscales, Negroes carrying roundels of hippopotamus hide and mounted on red asses, and golden-skinned Indians brandishing broadswords brighter than mirrors above their diadems. He conquered the Troglodytes and the Anthropophagi. He travelled across lands so hot that men's hair caught fire like torches in the burning sun, others so cold that their arms dropped off and fell to the ground, and yet others so foggy that they walked about surrounded by phantoms.

Republics in difficulties consulted him. At interviews with ambassadors he obtained unhoped-for terms. If a monarch behaved too badly, Julian would suddenly arrive and remonstrate with him. He liberated subject peoples. He freed queens shut up in prison towers. It was he and no other who slew the Viper of Milan and the Dragon of Oberbirbach.

Now the Emperor of Occitania, having defeated the Spanish Moors, had taken the sister of the Caliph of Córdoba as his concubine, and he had a daughter by her whom he had brought up as a Christian. But the Caliph, pretending that he wished to be converted, visited him with a great escort, massacred his entire garrison, and threw him into the deepest of dungeons, where he was treated very harshly in the hope of extorting his treasures from him.

Julian rushed to his aid, destroyed the infidel army, laid siege to the city, killed the Caliph, cut off his head, and tossed it over the ramparts like a ball. Then he released the Emperor from his prison and set him on his throne again in the presence of his assembled court.

As a reward for so great a service, the Emperor presented him with a number of baskets containing an immense fortune. Julian would not take them. Thinking that he wanted more money, the Emperor offered him three-quarters of his wealth. Again Julian refused. Then he offered to share his kingdom with him, and once more Julian declined. The Emperor was weeping with vexation, not knowing how to show his gratitude, when suddenly he slapped his forehead and whispered in a courtier's ear. The arras curtains were drawn aside and a girl appeared.

Her great dark eyes shone like two soft lights and her lips were parted in a delightful smile. The ringlets of her hair had caught on the jewels of her open-necked robe, and her transparent tunic hinted at the youthfulness of her body. She was dainty, round-cheeked, and slender-waisted.

Julian was dazzled with love for her, the more so because till then he had led a very chaste life.

So he took the Emperor's daughter in marriage, together with a castle which she had from her mother; and when the wedding festivities were over, and countless courtesies had been exchanged, bride and groom set off for their new home.

It was a palace of white marble in the Moorish style, built on a promontory in a grove of orange-trees. Terraces covered with flowers went down to the edge of a bay, where pink shells crackled underfoot. Behind the castle there stretched a forest in the shape of a fan. The sky was forever blue, and the trees swayed gently in the sea breeze or in the wind from the mountains which bounded on the distant horizon.

The rooms were full of shadow, but received some light from the inlaid decoration of the walls. Tall columns, as slender as reeds, supported the domes, which were adorned with reliefs imitating the stalactites which are to be found in grottoes.

There were fountains in the main rooms, mosaics in the courtyards, festooned walls, countless architectural refinements, and everywhere a silence so profound that one could hear the rustle of a scarf or the echo of a sigh.

Julian went no more to war. He rested in the midst of a people at peace, and every day a crowd passed before him, genuflecting and kissing his hands in the Eastern fashion.

Dressed in purple, he would remain for hours in a window-recess, leaning on the ledge and calling to mind his hunting days. He would have liked to be racing across the desert after the gazelle and the ostrich, stalking the leopard through the bamboo-canes, crossing forests teeming with rhinoceros, climbing the most inaccessible peaks to take better aim at the eagle, or fighting the white bear on drift-ice floating in the sea.

Sometimes, in a dream, he would see himself like our father Adam in the middle of Paradise, with all the birds and beasts around him; and stretching out his arm, he would put them to death. Or else they would file past him, two by two, according to size, from the elephants and lions down to the stoats and ducks, as they did on the day they entered Noah's ark. From the shadow of a cave he would hurl javelins at them which never missed their aim, but others would follow them, there would be no end to the slaughter, and he would wake up with his eyes rolling wildly.

Some princes among his friends invited him to go hunting

with them. He always refused, in the belief that by this kind of penance he would avert his evil destiny, for it seemed to him that the fate of his parents was bound up with the killing of animals. But it grieved him not to see anything of them, and this other longing of his became well-nigh unbearable.

His wife sent for jugglers and dancers to amuse him. She would go out with him into the country in an open litter; at other times they would lie in a boat, watching the fish darting about in water as clear as the sky. Often she would throw flowers in his face, or crouch at his feet drawing melodies from a three-stringed mandolin. Then, laying her clasped hand on his shoulder, she would ask shyly: 'What ails you, my dear lord?'

He would not answer, or would burst out sobbing. But at last one day he told her of his dreadful fear.

She fought against it, reasoning very soundly: his father and mother were probably dead, but if he were ever to see them again, what chance or purpose could possibly lead him to commit such a horrible crime? His fear was completely groundless, and he ought to take up hunting again.

Julian smiled as he listened to her, but could not make up his mind to satisfy his desire.

One evening in August when they were in their room, she had just got into bed, and he was kneeling down to say his prayers, when he heard the bark of a fox, followed by some light footsteps under the window. In the half-light he saw what appeared to be animal forms. The temptation was too strong for him and he took down his quiver from the wall.

She looked surprised.

'I am obeying your orders,' he said. 'I shall be back at sunrise.'

However, she feared some disaster. He reassured her and went out, astonished at her inconsistency.

Shortly afterwards a page came to tell her that two strangers, in the absence of the lord of the castle, were asking to see the lady.

And soon an old man and an old woman came into the room, bowed and dusty, dressed in coarse linen, and each leaning on a stick.

Plucking up courage, they explained that they brought Julian news of his parents.

She bent down to hear what they had to tell, but after exchanging glances they asked her if he still loved them and if he ever spoke of them.

'Oh, yes!' she said.

'Well, we are they!' they cried, and they sat down, being very tired and weary.

The young wife was far from being convinced that her husband was their son, but they gave her proof by describing certain special marks on his skin.

She jumped out of bed, called her page, and had a meal set before them.

Although they were very hungry, they could scarcely eat anything; and watching them, she noticed how their bony hands shook as they lifted their goblets.

They asked her countless questions about Julian. She answered every one, but was careful not to mention the gloomy obsession in which they were concerned.

When he had shown no sign of returning home, they had left their castle and they had been travelling now for several years, following up vague clues without ever losing hope. So much money had been required for river tolls and hostelry charges, to settle the dues of princes and satisfy the demands of robbers, that their purses were quite empty and they were now reduced to beggary. But what did that matter, when soon they would be embracing their son? They extolled his good fortune in having such a charming wife, and never tired of gazing at her and kissing her.

The sumptuousness of the room greatly astonished them, and the old man, after examining the walls, asked why they were decorated with the coat of arms of the Emperor of Occitania.

'He is my father,' she replied.

At that he started, remembering the gipsy's prophecy, while the old woman thought of the hermit's words. No doubt her son's high estate was only a foretaste of the eternal glory that lay before him. And both parents sat open-mouthed in the light of the candelabrum on the table.

They must have been very handsome in their youth. The mother had not lost any of her hair, which hung in thin tresses to the bottom of her cheeks, like strips of snow. The father, with his tall build and his great beard, looked like a statue in a church.

Julian's wife advised them not to wait up for him. She installed them in her own bed and shut the window. They fell asleep. Day was about to dawn, and the little birds had begun singing outside.

Julian had crossed the park and was walking through the forest with a springy step, enjoying the softness of the turf and the mildness of the air.

The shadows of the trees lay across the moss. Here and there the moon made white patches in the clearings, and he would pause, thinking he saw a pool of water, or else the surface of still ponds blending with the colour of the grass. Everywhere there was a great silence, and he could see none of the animals which a few minutes earlier had been prowling round his castle.

The forest became thicker and the darkness deeper. Puffs of warm air, heavy with enervating scents, went by him. He kept sinking into heaps of dead leaves, and leant against an oak to get his breath back.

Suddenly, from behind his back, a darker shape leapt forward – a wild boar. Julian had no time to take hold of his bow, and he was as distressed by this as if he had suffered some misfortune.

Then, when he had come out of the forest, he saw a wolf moving along beside a hedge. He shot an arrow at it. The wolf stopped, turned its head to look at him, and went on its way. It trotted on, always at the same distance, stopping from time to time and then, as soon as he took aim, continuing its flight.

In this way Julian crossed an endless plain and then some sandhills, and finally found himself on a plateau dominating a great stretch of country. Flat stones were strewn about among ruined burial vaults. He kept stumbling over dead men's bones; here and there worm-eaten crosses leaned over in a pitiful way. But suddenly something moved in the vague shadows around the tombs, and some hyenas sprang out, frightened and panting. Their claws tapped on the stones as they came up close to sniff at him, baring their fangs and showing their gums. He drew his sword, and at once they scattered in all directions, keeping up their headlong, limping gallop until they disappeared from view in a cloud of dust.

An hour later he met a mad bull in a ravine. Its horns were lowered and it was pawing the sand. Julian thrust his lance at it under the dewlap. The lance was shivered to pieces, as if the animal were made of bronze; and he closed his eyes, expecting to be killed. When he opened them again, the bull had vanished.

Then his very soul was overcome with shame. Realizing that some higher power was rendering his strength ineffective, he went back into the forest to make his way home.

His path was choked with creepers, and he was cutting them with his sword when a marten suddenly slipped between his legs, a panther leapt over his shoulder, and a snake wound its way up an ash-tree.

Among the leaves was a huge jackdaw, looking down at Julian, and here and there between the branches there appeared a host of gleaming lights, as if the sky had rained down all its stars into the forest. They were the eyes of animals – wild cats, squirrels, owls, parrots, monkeys.

Julian shot his arrows at them, and the feathered shafts settled on the leaves like white butterflies. He threw stones at them, and the stones fell to the ground without touching anything. He cursed out loud, spoiling for a fight, howling imprecations, choking with rage.

And all the animals he had hunted reappeared and formed a narrow ring around him. Some sat on their haunches; the others stood erect. He remained in the middle, numb with terror, incapable of making the slightest movement. By a supreme effort of will he took one step forward. The creatures in the trees spread their wings, those on the ground stirred their limbs, and all accompanied him.

The hyenas went in front, the wolf and the wild boar behind. The bull, on his right, swung its head from side to side, and on his left the snake slithered through the grass, while the panther, arching its back, advanced with great velvet-footed strides. He walked as slowly as possible so as not to irritate them, and as he went he saw porcupines, foxes, vipers, jackals, and bears emerging from the depths of the undergrowth.

He broke into a run, and they ran too. The snake hissed, and the foul beasts slavered. The wild boar prodded his heels with its tusks, and the wolf pushed its hairy muzzle into the palms of his hands. The monkeys pinched him and made faces at him; the marten rolled on his feet. A bear knocked his hat off with its paw, and the panther disdainfully dropped an arrow it was carrying in its mouth.

A certain irony was discernible in their sly behaviour; and as they watched him out of the corner of their eyes, they seemed to be thinking out a plan of revenge. Deafened by the insects' buzzing, bruised by the birds' tails, and suffocated by the animals' breath, he walked on with his arms outstretched and his eyes shut, like a blind man, without even the strength to cry for mercy.

The crow of a cock rang through the air and other cocks answered. It was day; and beyond the orange-trees he recognized the roof of his palace.

Then, at the edge of a field, only three paces away, he saw some red partridges fluttering about in the stubble. He unfastened his cloak and threw it over them like a net. When he uncovered them he found only one there, and that had been dead a long time and was decomposing.

This disappointment exasperated him more than all the others. His lust for blood took hold of him again, and since animals were lacking he would gladly have slaughtered men.

He climbed the three terraces and burst open the door with a blow of his fist, but at the foot of the stairs the thought of his beloved wife softened his heart. She was probably asleep. He decided to take her by surprise.

Removing his sandals, he turned the lock gently and went in.

The leaded window-panes dimmed the pale light of dawn. Julian's feet caught in some clothes lying on the floor, and a little farther on he knocked against a side-table which was still laden with dishes. 'She must have had something to eat', he thought, and he went on towards the bed, which was hidden in darkness at the far end of the room. He came up beside it, and to kiss his wife, bent down over the pillow where the two heads were lying side by side. Then he felt the touch of a beard against his mouth.

He started back, thinking he was going mad, but returned to the bedside, groping about until his fingers came across some long tresses of hair. To convince himself he was mistaken, he passed his hand slowly over the pillow again. This time there was no doubt it was a beard, and a man – a man sleeping with his wife!

In a burst of uncontrollable rage he plunged his dagger into their bodies, stamping his feet, foaming at the mouth, and roaring like a wild beast. Then he stopped. The two victims, pierced through the heart, had not even moved. He listened closely to the rattle of their dying breath, which came almost in unison, and as it grew fainter another in the distance took it up. Vague at first, this plaintive, long-drawn voice came nearer, grew louder, took on a cruel note; and to his horror he recognized the belling of the great black stag.

As he turned round, he thought he saw his wife's ghost framed in the doorway, with a light in her hand.

The noise of the murder had brought her to the spot. With one all-embracing glance she took everything in, and fled in horror, dropping her torch.

He picked it up.

His father and mother lay before him, stretched out on their backs with holes in their breasts; and their faces, serene and majestic, looked as though they were keeping some eternal secret. There were splashes and pools of blood on their white skin, on the bedclothes and the floor, and trickling down an ivory crucifix which hung in the alcove. The sun caught the stained-glass window at that moment, casting a crimson glow over the red splashes and multiplying them all over the room.

Julian went up to the two bodies, telling himself, and trying to believe, that this could not be true, that he must be mistaken, that one sometimes came across remarkable likenesses. Finally he bent forward slightly to look at the old man at close quarters, and between the half-closed eyelids he saw a glazed pupil which burnt through him like fire. Then he went to the other side of the bed where the other body lay, its white hair covering part of the face. Julian slipped his fingers under the tresses of hair and raised the head. He gazed at it, supporting it at arm's length with one hand and holding up the torch in the other. Drops of blood were oozing from the mattress and falling one by one on the floor.

At the end of the day he appeared before his wife, and in a voice quite unlike his own commanded her first of all not to answer him, come near him, or even look at him, but to carry out under pain of damnation all his orders, which were irrevocable.

The funeral rites were to be performed in accordance with the written instructions he had left on a *prie-dieu* in the mortuary chamber. He made over to her his palace, his vassals, and all his possessions, not excepting even his clothes or his sandals, which would be found at the head of the stairs.

She had done God's will in providing the occasion of his crime, and now she should pray for his soul, since from that day onwards he ceased to exist.

The dead were buried with great pomp in a monastery church three days' journey from the castle. A monk whose cowl was pulled down over his face followed the procession, but he stayed at some distance from the others, and no one dared to speak to him.

During the Mass he remained prone in the centre of the doorway, his arms stretched out in the form of a cross, and his forehead in the dust.

After the burial he was seen to take the road leading to the mountains. He turned to look back several times, and finally disappeared.

3

HE went his way, begging for his daily bread all over the world.

He would hold out his hand to riders on the high roads, bend his knee before harvesters, or stand motionless at courtyard gates, and his face was so sad that no one ever refused him alms.

In a spirit of humility he would tell his story, and then everyone would flee from him, making the sign of the cross. In the villages he had passed through before, he was no sooner recognized than people shut their doors, shouted threats, or threw stones at him. The most charitable of them would put a bowl of soup on their window-sills and then close the shutters so as not to see him.

Rebuffed on all sides, he shunned mankind, and fed on roots, plants, wild fruit, and shell-fish which he looked for along the seashore.

Sometimes, rounding a hill, he saw beneath him a jumble of roofs crowded together, with stone spires, bridges, towers, and a network of dark streets from which a continual murmur rose to his ears.

The craving to take part in the life of other men impelled him to go down into the city. But the bestial faces of the people he met, the noise of their work, and the triviality of their conversation froze his heart. On feast-days, when the sound of the great cathedral bells filled everyone with joy from daybreak onwards, he would watch the townspeople coming out of their houses, the dancing in the squares, the beer-fountains at the crossroads, the damask awnings in front of princely homes; and in the evening, through ground-floor windows, the long family tables where grandparents dandled little children on their knees. Sobs choked him, and he would turn away back to the open country.

He felt pangs of love as he gazed at foals in the meadows, birds in their nests, and insects on the flowers. But at his approach they all ran farther off, hid in terror, or flew swiftly away.

He sought out lonely places. But the wind would sound in his ears like the rattle of a death-agony. The dew falling on the ground would recall other, heavier drops. The sun, every evening, would splash blood across the clouds, and each night in his dreams the murder of his parents would begin all over again.

He made himself a hair-shirt with iron spikes. He climbed on his knees every hill which had a chapel at the top. But the pitiless thought dimmed the glory of the shrines, and tortured him even in his acts of mortification.

He did not rebel against God for having imposed this deed on him, and yet the idea that he could have committed it reduced him to despair.

His own body was so repulsive to him that in the hope of freeing himself from it, he risked it in perilous enterprises. He saved paralytics from fires and children from yawning chasms. The abyss cast him up; the flames spared him.

Time did not ease his sufferings. It became so intolerable that he resolved to die.

And one day when he was standing beside a pool, bending over it to gauge the depth of the water, he saw before him a gaunt old man, with a white beard and a face so sad that Julian could not restrain his tears. The other wept too. Without recognizing his own reflection, he vaguely remembered having seen a face like this before. Then he gave a cry – it was his father; and he thought no more of killing himself.

So, bearing the burden of his memories, he travelled through many lands, until he came to a river which was dangerous to cross because of the strong current and the great stretch of mud along its banks. No one for a long time past had dared to try to cross it.

An old boat had been left among the reeds, with its stern buried in the mud and its bows up in the air. Julian examined it and found a pair of oars, and he was struck by the thought of spending his life in the service of others.

He began by making a kind of causeway on the bank so that

people could get down to the stream. He broke his nails moving the huge stones, carried them pressed against his belly, slipped in the mud, sank into it, and several times came near to death. Next he mended the boat with bits of wreckage, and built himself a hut out of tree-trunks and clay.

Once the ferry became known, travellers appeared. They signalled to him from the other side by waving flags, and Julian promptly jumped into his boat. It was very heavy, and they overloaded it with all sorts of packs and bundles, not to mention the beasts of burden, which added to the confusion by lashing out in fright. Julian asked nothing for his labour; some gave him scraps of food from their wallets or worn-out clothes they did not want any longer. Some brutish ruffians would shout curses at him. Julian remonstrated gently with them, only to be answered with abuse. He contented himself with giving them his blessing.

A little table, a stool, a bed of dead leaves, and three clay cups were all the furniture he had. Two holes in the wall served as windows. One one side, as far as the eye could see, stretched barren plains dotted here and there with pale meres, while in front of him the greenish waters of the great river rolled by. In spring the damp earth gave out an odour of decay. Then a blustering wind would raise clouds of dust which penetrated everywhere, muddying the water and leaving grit in his mouth. A little later it was the turn of clouds of mosquitoes, whose humming and stinging went on night and day. And after that came dreadful frosts which made everything as hard as stone and inspired a frantic craving for meat.

Months went by when Julian saw no one. Often he would close his eyes and try to recapture his youth in memory. The courtyard of the castle would appear before him, with greyhounds on the steps, pages in the armoury, and a fair-haired boy under a vine-covered arbour, between an old man wrapped in furs and a lady with a great coif. And suddenly the two corpses were there. He would throw himself flat on his bed, weeping and crying 'Ah, poor father! Poor mother, poor mother!' And he would fall into a fitful slumber in which these funereal visions continued to haunt him.

One night, while he was asleep, he thought he heard someone calling him. He strained his ears, but could make out nothing but the roar of the waves.

But again the same voice called out:

'Julian!'

It came from the far bank, and this struck him as extraordinary, considering the width of the river.

A third time the summons came:

'Julian!'

And this penetrating voice had the sound of a church-bell.

Lighting his lantern, Julian left the hut. A raging tempest was blowing through the night. The darkness was profound, broken only here and there by the whiteness of the leaping waves.

After a moment's hesitation Julian cast off the painter. At once the water became calm, and the boat glided across it to the other bank, where a man was waiting.

He was wrapped in a ragged cloth, his face like a plaster mask and his two eyes redder than burning coals. Holding the lantern up to him, Julian saw that he was covered with a hideous leprosy, and yet there was something kingly in his bearing.

As soon as he got into the boat, it went a long way down in the water, under the weight of his body; then it rose again with a jolt, and Julian started rowing.

At every stroke the surf lifted the bows up in the air. The water, looking blacker than ink, streamed furiously past on either side. It hollowed out abysses and built up mountains, and the boat leapt up before sinking again into the depths, where it spun round, tossed by the wind.

Julian bent his body, stretched his arms out, and arched himself backwards from his feet to get more power. The hail lashed his hands, the rain ran down his back, the violence of the wind took his breath away, and at last he stopped. The boat then began drifting away downstream. But realizing that this was a matter of the first importance, a trust he must on no account desert, he took up his oars again, and the rattle of the rowlocks cut through the clamour of the storm.

The little lantern was shining in front of him. Birds fluttering past it hid it from time to time. But all the while he could see the eyes of the Leper, who stood in the stern of the boat, motionless as a pillar.

And this went on for a long, long time.

When they reached the hut, Julian shut the door and saw the Leper sitting on the stool. The shroud-like garment which covered him had slipped down to his hips, and his shoulders, his chest, and his scrawny arms were hidden under patches of scaly pustules. His brow was furrowed with enormous wrinkles. Like a skeleton he had a hole where the nose should have been, and from his bluish lips came a nauseous breath as thick as a fog.

'I am hungry,' he said.

Julian gave him what he had: an old gammon of bacon and the crust from a loaf of black bread.

When he had finished eating, the table, the bowl, and the handle of the knife bore the same marks that could be seen on his body.

Next he said: 'I am thirsty.'

Julian went to get his pitcher, and as he picked it up, there arose from it a scent which made his heart and nostrils expand. It was wine. What a wonderful find this was, he thought. But the Leper stretched out his hand and emptied the whole pitcher at one draught.

Then he said: 'I am cold.'

With his candle Julian set light to a bundle of bracken in the middle of the hut.

The Leper came near to warm himself. Squatting on his heels, he began trembling all over. His strength was flagging, his eyes had stopped shining, his sores were running, and in an almost inaudible voice he murmured : 'Your bed!'

Julian tenderly helped him to drag himself to it, even spreading the sail of his boat over him to cover him.

The Leper lay there groaning. His teeth showed at the corners of his mouth, his chest heaved as his dying breath came more and more quickly, and at every gasp his belly was sucked in as far as his backbone.

Then he closed his eyes.

'My bones are like ice. Come here beside me!'

And Julian, lifting the sail, lay down side by side with him on the dead leaves.

The Leper turned his head.

'Take off your clothes so that I may feel the warmth of your body!'

Julian stripped, and then, naked as on the day he was born, he lay down on the bed again. And against his thigh he felt the Leper's skin, colder than a snake and as rough as a file.

He spoke encouragingly to him, and the other gasped out in reply :

'Ah, I am dying! Come closer and warm me! No, not with your hands, with your whole body!'

Julian stretched himself out on top of him, mouth to mouth, breast to breast.

Then the Leper clasped him in his arms. And all at once his eyes took on the brightness of the stars, his hair spread out like the rays of the sun, and the breath of his nostrils had the sweetness of roses. A cloud of incense rose from the hearth and the waves outside began to sing.

Meanwhile an abundance of delight, a superhuman joy

swept like a flood into Julian's soul as he lay there in a swoon. And the one whose arms still held him tight grew and grew, until his head and his feet touched the walls of the hut. The roof flew off, the heavens unfolded – and Julian rose towards the blue, face to face with Our Lord Jesus Christ, who bore him up to Heaven.

And that is the story of St Julian Hospitator, more or less as it is depicted on a stained-glass window in a church in my part of the world.

Herodias

I

THE citadel of Machaerus stood to the east of the Dead Sea, on a cone-shaped basalt peak. It was surrounded by four deep valleys, one at each side, another in front, and the fourth behind. There were houses huddled together at its base, encircled by a wall which went up and down with the uneven ground; and a zigzag road hewn out of the rock linked the town with the fortress, whose walls were a hundred and twenty cubits high, with a good many angles, battlements along the edge, and here and there towers which looked like floral ornaments on this crown of stone suspended over the abyss.

Inside the walls was a palace embellished with porticoes and roofed over with a terrace, and this terrace was enclosed by a sycamore balustrade fitted with poles for an awning.

One morning, before daybreak, the Tetrarch Herod Antipas came out to lean on it and look around.

Immediately beneath him, the mountains were beginning to unveil their crests, though their main bulk, down to the chasms below, was still in shadow. A drifting mist broke up to reveal the outline of the Dead Sea. The sun, rising behind Machaerus, sent out a reddish glow, which gradually lit up the sands of the foreshore, the hills, the desert, and farther off all the mountains of Judea, with their rugged grey slopes. Engedi drew a black line across the centre, while in the background there rose the dome-like silhouette of Hebron. There was Eschol with its pomegranates, Sorek with its vines, Karmel with its fields of sesame, and, dominating Jerusalem, the huge cube-shaped tower of Antonia. The Tetrarch looked away from it to gaze at the palm-trees of Jericho on his right, and he thought of the other towns in his Galilee – Capernaum, Endor, Nazareth, and Tiberias – which he would perhaps never see again. The Jordan flowed on across the arid plain, which was as dazzling white as a sheet of snow. The lake now looked as if it were made of lapis lazuli, and at its southernmost point, towards the Yemen, Antipas recognized something he had been afraid to see. Brown tents were scattered here and there, men with lances were moving among their horses, and dying fires shone like sparks on the ground.

They were the troops of the King of the Arabs, whose daughter he had divorced to take Herodias, the wife of one of his brothers who lived in Italy and had no pretensions to power.

Antipas was waiting for help from the Romans, consumed with anxiety because Vitellius, the Governor of Syria, was a long time coming.

Agrippa, he thought, had probably discredited him with the Emperor. His third brother, Philip, sovereign of Batanea, was secretly arming. The Jews had had enough of his idolatrous ways, and everyone else of his rule, so that he was hesitating between two possible courses: to conciliate the Arabs or to conclude an alliance with the Parthians. On the pretext of celebrating his birthday, he had invited the commanders of his troops, the stewards of his estates, and the chief men of Galilee to a great banquet that very day.

He scanned all the roads with a piercing eye. They were deserted. Some eagles flew overhead; the soldiers along the ramparts were asleep against the walls; nothing stirred inside the castle.

Suddenly a voice in the distance, which sounded as if it came from the depths of the earth, made the Tetrarch turn pale. He leant forward to listen; it had stopped. Then it came again. Clapping his hands, he called out:

'Mannaëi! Mannaëi!'

A man appeared, naked to the waist like the masseurs at the baths. He was very tall, old, and gaunt, and he wore a sword in a bronze sheath at his side. His hair, drawn back with a comb, made his forehead seem higher than it was. Drowsiness dulled his eyes, but his teeth shone and his toes trod lightly on the flagstones; his body was as supple as a monkey's, his face as impassive as a mummy's.

'Where is he?' asked the Tetrarch.

Pointing with his thumb to something behind them, Mannaëi answered:

'Still there.'

And Antipas, heaving a sigh of relief, inquired about Jokanaan, whom the Latins call St John the Baptist. Had anything more been seen of those two men who had been admitted to his cell the other month as a favour, and had the reason for their visit been discovered?

Mannaëi replied:

'They exchanged some mysterious words with him, like thieves when they meet at crossroads in the evening. Then they went off towards Upper Galilee, saying that they would return with great tidings.'

Antipas bowed his head and then, with a horror-stricken look, cried out:

'Guard him! Guard him well! And let no one in! Make fast the door and cover the pit! Nobody must even suspect he is alive!'

Mannaëi had already carried out these orders before they were given, for Jokanaan was a Jew, and like all Samaritans he loathed the Jews.

Their temple at Gerizim, which Moses had intended to be the centre of Israel, had been lost to them since the reign of Hyrcanus, and the Temple at Jerusalem roused them to fury, as an outrage and a standing injustice. Mannaëi had once entered it secretly to pollute the altar with dead men's bones; his companions, who were not as swift-footed as he, had been beheaded.

He caught sight of it in the gap between two hills. The white marble of its walls and the gold plating of its roof shone brightly in the sun. It was like a luminous mountain, something superhuman, crushing everything else under its opulence and its arrogance.

Then he stretched out his arms towards Zion, and, standing upright, with his head thrown back and his fists clenched, he hurled a curse at it, convinced that his words would have their effect.

Antipas listened and gave no sign of being shocked.

The Samaritan went on:

'Now and then he becomes restive, he wants to get out, and he hopes to be set free. At other times he is as quiet as a sick animal. Or else I see him walking up and down in the dark, saying over and over again: "What does it matter? If He is to wax, then I must wane!"'

Antipas and Mannaëi looked at each other. But the Tetrarch was weary of reflection.

All these mountains around him, like great waves petrified in layers, the black chasms in the sides of the cliffs, the immensity of the blue sky, and cruel brilliance of the morning light, and the depth of the abysses disturbed him, and his spirits sank as he gazed at the desert, with its ragged contours looking like the ruins of amphitheatres and palaces. The hot wind carried a smell of sulphur, like the stench of the accursed cities buried under the banks of the heavy waters. These tokens of an immortal anger struck terror into his thoughts, and he stayed there with his elbows on the balustrade, his eyes staring, and his forehead in his hands. Someone touched him. He turned round. Herodias stood before him.

She was wrapped in a light purple simar which reached down to her sandals. She had left her room in a hurry and was wearing neither necklaces nor ear-rings; a tress of her dark hair hung down over one arm, and the end of it disappeared between her breasts. Her wide nostrils were quivering; her face was radiant with the joy of victory; and, shaking the Tetrarch she shouted:

'Caesar is our friend! Agrippa is in prison!'

'Who told you so?'

'I know it!'

She added: 'It is because he wanted Caius to be Emperor!'

While living on their charity, Agrippa had been trying to obtain the title of king, which they coveted just as much as he did. But in future they would have no cause for fear.

'The dungeons of Tiberius are hard to open,' said Herodias, 'and life inside them is sometimes far from safe!'

Antipas understood what she meant, and although she was Agrippa's sister, her dreadful scheme seemed to him to be justified. Murders of this kind were in the natural order of events and happened in all royal houses. In Herod's, they had lost count of them.

Then she told him all that she had done: how Agrippa's clients had been bribed, his letters opened, and spies posted at every door, and how she had managed to seduce Eutychus the informer.

'It was nothing', she said. 'Have I not done more for you before? Have I not given up my daughter?'

After her divorce she had left this child in Rome, confident that she would have others by the Tetrarch. She never spoke of her, and he wondered what could be the reason for this sudden display of emotion.

The awning had been opened out and big cushions hurriedly placed beside them. Herodias sank down on them, and, turning her back to him, began to cry. Then she passed her hand over her eyes, saying that she did not want to think about it any more, and that she was perfectly happy. And she reminded him of their talks back there in the atrium, their meetings at the baths, their walks along the Via Sacra, and their evenings together in the great villas, by murmuring fountains and under floral arches, with the Roman Campagna spread out before them. She looked at him as she used to in the old days, rubbing herself gently against his breast, with coaxing, caressing gestures.

He pushed her away. The love which she was trying to revive was so far away now! And it was the cause of all his misfortunes, for the war had been going on now for nearly twelve years. It had aged the Tetrarch. His shoulders, under the dark, violet-edged toga, were bent with care; his white hair mingled with his beard; and the sunshine which came through the awning lit up his wrinkled brow. Herodias's brow was wrinkled too, and the two of them sat face to face, looking at each other with angry eyes.

The mountain roads began to fill with people. There were herdsmen goading oxen, children pulling donkeys, grooms leading horses. Those coming down from the heights beyond Machaerus disappeared behind the castle; others climbed the ravine in front and unloaded their burdens in the courtyards when they reached the town. These were the Tetrarch's purveyors, and servants sent on ahead by his guests.

Then, at the end of the terrace, on the left an Essene appeared, white-robed and barefoot, with a stoic air about him. Mannaëi rushed forward from the right, brandishing his sword.

Herodias called out: 'Kill him!'

'Stop!' cried the Tetrarch.

He halted in his tracks, and so did the other. Then they withdrew by different staircases, walking backwards and keeping each other in sight.

'I know that man', said Herodias. 'His name is Phanuel, and

94

he is trying to see Jokanaan, whom you are foolish enough to keep alive.'

Antipas retorted that he might be of use some day. His attacks on Jerusalem were bringing the rest of the Jews over to their side.

'No!' she replied. 'They accept any master they are given, and are incapable of making a country of their own.' As for Jokanaan, who was stirring up the people with hopes cherished since the days of Nehemiah, the best policy was to get rid of him.

There was no hurry, said the Tetrarch, and it was nonsense to think that Jokanaan was dangerous. He gave a forced laugh.

'Be quiet!' she said. And once again she told him how she had been humiliated one day when she was on her way to Gilead for the balsam harvest.

'Some people were putting their clothes on beside the river. On a mound nearby a man was speaking. He was wearing a camel-skin about his loins and his head was like the head of a lion. As soon as he saw me he spat all the curses of the prophets at me. His eyes flashed, his voice roared, and he raised his arms as if to pluck thunder out of the sky. It was impossible to get away from him. The wheels of my chariot were up to their axles in sand, and I moved off slowly, cowering under my cloak, my blood running cold at the insults that were raining down on me.'

Jokanaan was a thorn in her side. The soldiers who had seized and bound him had been given orders to stab him if he resisted: he had been meek and submissive. They had put snakes in his prison: the snakes had died.

The futility of these stratagems exasperated Herodias. Besides, why was he fighting her, and what did he stand to gain by it? The speeches he had addressed to great crowds had spread far and wide, and were still circulating; she heard them repeated everywhere, and they filled the air. Faced with legions of troops, she would have been brave enough, but this intangible force was deadlier than the sword, and utterly perplexing. White with anger, she paced up and down the terrace, at a loss for words to express the emotions that stifled her.

She was also troubled by the thought that the Tetrarch might give way to public opinion and decide to repudiate her. Then all would be lost! Ever since childhood she had nursed the dream of a great empire. It was to gain it that she had left her first husband for this one, who she now thought had duped her.

'I provided myself with a fine support when I entered your family!'

'It is as good as yours', said the Tetrarch simply.

Herodias felt the blood of ancestral priests and kings boiling in her veins.

'But your grandfather was a sweeper in the Temple of Askalon, and the others were just a horde of shepherds, robbers, and caravaneers, vassals of Judah ever since the days of King David! My ancestors have all beaten yours in battle. The first of the Maccabees chased you out of Hebron, and Hyrcanus forced you to be circumcised!'

And breathing out all the contempt of the patrician for the plebeian, the hatred of Jacob for Edom, she reproached him with his indifference to insults, his leniency towards the Pharisees who were betraying him, and his cowardice in the face of the people who detested him.

'You are just like them – admit it! And you miss that Arab girl dancing round the stones. Take her back, then! Go and live with her under her canvas roof, eat the bread she has baked under the ashes, swallow the curdled milk of her ewes, kiss her blue cheeks, and forget about me!'

The Tetrarch was no longer listening. He was looking at a house with a flat roof, on which he could see a girl and an old woman, who was holding a parasol with a reed handle as long as a fisherman's rod. In the middle of the carpet a big travelling basket lay open, overflowing with girdles, veils, and jewelled pendants. Now and then the girl bent over these things and shook them in the air. She was dressed like Roman girls, in a pleated tunic and a peplum with emerald tassels; blue fillets bound her hair, which was doubtless too heavy, for she put her hand up to it from time to time. The shadow of the parasol moved about over her, partly hiding her from view. Two or three times Antipas caught a glimpse of her delicate neck, the corner of an eye, the curve of a little mouth. But he could see the whole of her figure, from the hips to the neck, bending and straightening with supple grace. He looked out for the repetition of this movement, and his breathing grew louder; flames kindled in his eyes. Herodias was watching him.

He asked: 'Who is she?'

She replied that she had no idea, and went away, her anger suddenly allayed.

Waiting for the Tetrarch under the porticoes were some Galileans, the chief scribe, the steward of the pastures, the manager of the salt mines, and a Babylonian Jew who was in command of his horsemen. All saluted him with one voice, and he disappeared in the direction of the inner rooms.

Phanuel appeared suddenly round the corner of a corridor.

'Ah, you again! I suppose you have come to see Jokanaan.'

'And to see you too! I have something important to tell you.'

And not letting Antipas out of his sight, he followed him into a dimly lit room.

Daylight filtered in through a grating which extended the entire length of the cornice. The walls were painted a garnet red that was almost black. At the far end of the room stood an ebony bed with ox-hide straps. A golden buckler above it shone like a sun.

Antipas went right across the room and lay down on the bed.

Phanuel remained standing. He raised his arm and said as one inspired:

'The Almighty sends us one of His sons from time to time. Jokanaan is one of these. If you ill-treat him, you will be punished.'

'But it is he who persecutes me!' cried Antipas. 'He asked me to do something which was quite impossible, and ever since then he has been plaguing me. And I was not hard on him to begin with! Why, he has even sent men from Machaerus who are turning my provinces upside down. Woe betide him! Since he attacks me, I defend myself!'

'He is too violent in his anger', replied Phanuel. 'But no matter, you must release him.'

'One does not release wild beasts', said the Tetrarch.

The Essene answered: 'Have no fear! He will go among the Arabs, the Gauls, and the Scythians. His work must extend to the ends of the earth!'

Antipas seemed lost in a trance.

'He has tremendous power . . . I cannot help liking him.'

'Then you will set him free?'

The Tetrarch shook his head. He was afraid of Herodias, of Mannaëi, of the unknown.

Phanuel tried to persuade him to change his mind, promising, as a guarantee of his plans, that the Essenes would make their submission to the Kings. People respected these poor men, dressed in flax, who defied torture and read the future in the stars.

Antipas remembered something Phanuel had said just before.

'What is this news you told me was so important?'

A Negro rushed in, his body white with dust. He was gasping for breath and all he could say was:

'Vitellius!'

'What? Is he coming?'

'I have seen him. He will be here within three hours!'

The curtains in the corridors were shaken as if by the wind.
A great din filled the castle: the noise of people running, furniture being dragged about, and silverware falling to the ground.
And from the tops of the towers trumpets sounded to warn the
scattered slaves.

2

THE ramparts were crowded with people when Vitellius entered
the courtyard. He was leaning on his interpreter's arm, and
wearing the toga, the laticlave, and the laced boots of a consul.
He was surrounded by lictors and followed by a large red litter
adorned with plumes and mirrors.

The lictors set against the gate their twelve fasces: rods
fastened by a strap, with a hatchet in the middle. At this everyone trembled before the majesty of the Roman people.

The litter, which eight men were carrying, came to a stop.
There stepped out of it a youth with a big paunch, a pimply
face, and rows of pearls on his fingers. They offered him a cup
full of wines and spices. He emptied it and called for another.

The Tetrarch had gone down on his knees to the Proconsul,
saying how distressed he was not to have known sooner that he
was to be favoured with his presence. Otherwise he would have
given orders that all the honours due to the Vitellii should be
paid to him on his way. They were descended from the goddess
Vitellia, and a road from the Janiculum to the sea still bore their
name. There were countless quaestorships and consulships in
their family, and as for Lucius, who was now his guest, thanks
were due to him as conqueror of the Clites and father of young
Aulus here, who might be said to be returning to his native

land, since the East was the home of the gods. These extrava-
gant compliments were uttered in Latin, and Vitellius accepted
them impassively.

He replied that the great Herod was himself enough to make
the glory of a nation. The Athenians had put him in charge of
the Olympic games. He had built temples in honour of Aug-
ustus, and he had been patient, ingenious, formidable, and stead-
fastly loyal to the Caesars.

Between the pillars with their bronze capitals Herodias could
be seen approaching with the air of an empress, surrounded by
women and eunuchs carrying burning incense on silver-gilt
salvers.

The Proconsul took three steps to meet her, and bowed his
head in greeting.

'How fortunate it is', she exclaimed, 'that henceforth Agrippa, the enemy of Tiberius, will find it impossible to do any
harm!'

Vitellius did not know what had happened and thought
Herodias seemed a dangerous woman. When Antipas began
swearing that he would do anything for the Emperor, he in-
terjected:

'Even if other people suffered in the process?'

He, Vitellius, had obtained hostages from the King of the
Parthians, but the Emperor had forgotten about it, for Antipas, who had been present at the conference and had wanted
to attract attention, had sent the news off straight away. Hence
the deep hatred Vitellius felt for him, and his delay in sending
him assistance.

The Tetrarch stammered out some excuses, but Aulus said
with a laugh:

'Calm down! I will protect you!'

The Proconsul pretended not to have heard. The father's
prospects depended on the son's iniquities, and this flower from
the mud of Capri brought him such immense benefits that he

lavished attention on it, while at the same time treating it with suspicion, because of the poison it contained.

A tumult arose under the gate. A string of white mules was being led in, ridden by men in the garb of priests. They were Sadducees and Pharisees, whom the same ambition brought to Machaerus, the former wanting to obtain the office of High Priest and the latter to keep it. Their faces were grim, especially those of the Pharisees, who were hostile to Rome and the Tetrarch. The skirts of their tunics hampered them in the throng, and their tiaras slipped about on their foreheads, on top of inscribed fillets of parchment.

Almost at the same time some soldiers of the advance-guard arrived. They had put their shields inside sacks, to protect them from the dust. Behind them came Marcellus, the Proconsul's lieutenant, with some publicans holding wooden tablets tucked under their arms.

Antipas presented the principal members of his suite: Tolmaï, Kanthera, Sehon, Ammonius of Alexandria, who bought asphalt for him, Naaman, captain of his velites, and Jacim the Babylonian.

Vitellius had noticed Mannaëi.

'That fellow there, what is he?'

The Tetrarch indicated with a gesture that he was the executioner.

Then he introduced the Sadducees.

Jonathas, a little man with a free and easy manner who spoke Greek, begged the master to honour them with a visit to Jerusalem. He replied that he would probably be going there.

Eleazer, a man with a hooked nose and a long beard, appealed on behalf of the Pharisees for the return of the High Priest's mantle held by the civil authority in the Antonia.

Then the Galileans denounced Pontius Pilate: because of a lunatic who had been hunting for David's golden vases in a cave near Samaria, he had killed some of the inhabitants. They all spoke at once, Mannaëi more passionately than the rest. Vitellius declared that the criminals would be punished.

Some shouting started in front of one of the porticoes, where the soldiers had hung their shields. Now that the coverings had been removed. Caesar's effigy could be seen on the bosses. This, to the Jews, was idolatry. Antipas harangued them, while Vitellius, installed on a raised seat in the colonnade, marvelled at their fury. Tiberius had done right to banish four hundred of them to Sardinia. But in their own country they were strong, and he ordered the shields to be taken down.

Then they swarmed round the Proconsul, begging for the redress of injustices, for privileges, for alms. Clothes were torn in the crush, and slaves with sticks hit out right and left to make room. Those nearest the gate began to go down the road, and then, as others came up it, fell back. There were two streams going to and fro in this swaying crowd, hemmed in by the surrounding walls.

Vitellius asked why there were so many people there. Antipas explained that it was for a banquet to celebrate his birthday, and he pointed to some of his servants who were leaning over the battlements and hauling up huge baskets of meat, fruit and vegetables, antelopes and storks, great blue fish, grapes, watermelons, and pomegranates heaped up in pyramids. It was too much for Aulus, who rushed off to the kitchens, carried away by that gluttony which was to astonish the whole world.

As he was going past one of the wine-cellars, he noticed some pots that were like breast-plates. Vitellius came and looked at them, and insisted on having the underground rooms in the fortress opened up for inspection.

These rooms were hewn out of the rock in the shape of high vaults, with pillars at regular intervals. The first contained old pieces of armour, but the second was crammed with pikes,

whose points stuck out of bunches of feathers. The third looked
as if it were lined with reed mats, the slender arrows in it were
stacked so straight and close together. Scimitar blades covered
the walls of the fourth. In the middle of the fifth were rows of
helmets, which, with their crests, looked like a battalion of red
serpents. In the sixth there was nothing but quivers to be seen,
in the seventh greaves, and in the eighth brassards; while in the
other rooms there were forks, grappling-irons, ladders, ropes,
and even poles for the catapults and bells for the dromedaries'
breast-plates. And as the mountain widened out towards its
base, hollowed out inside like a beehive, there were still more
and even deeper rooms under these.

Vitellius, Phineas his interpreter, and Sisenna the chief publican, went through them by the light of torches held by three
eunuchs.

In the semi-darkness they could make out hideous objects in-
vented by the barbarians: clubs studded with nails, poisoned
javelins, and pincers like crocodiles' jaws. In fact, the Tetrarch
had sufficient munitions of war in Machaerus to equip forty
thousand men.

He had gathered them together in case his enemies formed
an alliance against him. But the Proconsul might believe, or
say, that they were for fighting the Romans, and so he began
casting about for an explanation. Perhaps he could say that
they were not his; that many of them were used to keep brig-
ands at bay; that some were needed against the Arabs; or else
that the whole stock had belonged to his father. And instead
of walking behind the Proconsul, he went striding on in front.
Then he placed himself against the wall, extending his arms
so that his toga hid part of it; but the top of a door showed
above his head. Vitellius saw it, and wanted to know what was
inside.

Only the Babylonian, he was told, could open it.

'Call the Babylonian!'

They waited for him.

His father had come from the banks of the Euphrates to offer himself and five hundred horsemen to Herod the Great, for the defence of the eastern frontiers. When the kingdom was divided, Jacim had stayed with Philip and was now in the service of Antipas.

He arrived with a bow across his shoulders and a whip in his hand. Multicoloured cords were wound tightly round his bandy legs. His bulging arms emerged from a sleeveless tunic and a fur bonnet shaded his face. His beard was curled in ringlets.

At first he did not seem to understand the interpreter, but Vitellius shot a glance at Antipas, who promptly repeated the order. Then Jacim placed both hands against the door, and it slid into the wall.

A breath of hot air came out of the darkness. A winding passage led downwards; they followed it, and eventually reached the threshold of a cavern which was larger than the other underground rooms. At the far end an archway opened on to the chasm which defended the citadel on that side. A honeysuckle clung to the roof, its flowers dangling in the sunlight. A thin trickle of water was purling across the floor.

There were perhaps a hundred white horses there, eating barley from a shelf on a level with their mouths. Their manes were all dyed blue, their hooves were enveloped in esparto mittens, and the hair between their ears was puffed out over their foreheads like a wig. They were lazily whisking their exceptionally long tails against their hocks. The Proconsul was struck dumb with admiration.

They were marvellous beasts, supple as snakes and light as birds. They would go off as swiftly as their rider's arrow, knock men down and bite them in the belly, make their way over rocky ground, leap across chasms, and keep up their headlong gallop over the plains for a whole day; a word would stop them.

As soon as Jacim went in they came up to him, like sheep at the approach of a shepherd; and stretching out their necks, they looked at him anxiously with child-like eyes. From force of habit he gave a hoarse, deep-throated cry which put them in good spirits, and they reared up, impatient to be out and away, begging for a gallop.

Antipas, fearing that Vitellius might take them away, had shut them up in this place, which was meant for animals in case of a siege.

'This is a poor stable,' said the Proconsul, and you run the risk of losing them. Make an inventory, Sisenna!'

The publican took a tablet from his girdle, counted the horses, and wrote down the number. The agents of the tax companies were in the habit of bribing governors in order to plunder their provinces. This man, with his weasel jaw and blinking eyes, nosed about everywhere.

At last they went up to the courtyard again.

There were round bronze lids set here and there in the middle of the paving-stones to cover the cisterns. Sisenna noticed one which was bigger than the rest and did not sound the same when they trod on it. He struck them all in turn and then, dancing up and down, shouted:

'I've found it! I've found it! Herod's treasure is here!'

Hunting for Herod's treasure was a mania with the Romans. The Tetrarch swore that there was no such thing. Then what was underneath?

'Nothing! A man, a prisoner.'

'Let us see him', said Vitellius.

The Tetrarch did not obey, for to do so would be to reveal his secret to the Jews. His unwillingness to lift the lid put Vitellius out of patience.

'Break it in!' he cried to the lictors.

Mannaëi had guessed what was claiming their attention. Seeing an axe, he thought that Jokanaan was going to be beheaded. He stopped the lictor at the first blow on the plate, inserted a kind of hook between it and the paving-stones, then, stiffening his long thin arms, raised it gently until it fell back. Everyone was filled with admiration for the old man's strength. Under the wood-lined cover was a trap-door of the same size, which fell open in two pieces when Mannaëi struck it with his fist. A hole was now revealed, an enormous pit with an unrailed staircase winding round it, and those who leaned over the edge saw at the bottom something vague and terrifying.

A human being lay there on the ground, his long hair entangled with the hair of the skin which covered his back. He got up. His forehead touched a grating fixed horizontally across the pit, and from time to time he disappeared into the depths of his lair.

The sun was glinting on the tips of the tiaras and the hilts of the swords, and making the pavement unbearably hot. Doves flew out from the friezes and wheeled over the courtyard: it was the time when Mannaëi usually threw them some grain. He was crouching in front of the Tetrarch, who stood close to Vitellius. The Galileans, the priests, and the soldiers formed a circle behind, and all were silent, anxiously waiting to see what would happen next.

First, in a sepulchral voice, there came a great sigh.

Herodias heard it at the other end of the palace. Yielding to an irresistible urge, she made her way through the crowd and bent forward to listen, resting one hand on Mannaëi's shoulder.

The voice rose, saying:

'Woe unto you, Pharisees and Sadducees, brood of vipers, swollen wineskins, tinkling cymbals!'

They recognized Jokanaan. His name was passed round, and more people came running up to listen.

'Woe unto you, O people! Woe unto the traitors of Judah

and the drunkards of Ephraim, unto those who live in the rich valley and are overcome by the fumes of wine! May they pass away like running water, like the snail that melts as it moves, like the aborted child that never sees the sun! Then, Moab, you shall have to hide in the cypresses like the sparrows and in the caves like the jerboas. The gates of your fortresses shall be broken more easily than nut-shells, the walls shall crumble, the cities shall burn, and the scourge of the Lord shall not cease. It shall tumble your limbs about in your blood, like wool in a dyer's vat. It shall tear you like a new harrow; it shall scatter all the morsels of your flesh upon the mountains!'

Of what conqueror was he speaking? Was it Vitellius? Only the Romans could produce such a holocaust. Protesting voices were raised: 'Enough, enough! Let him be silent!'

He went on in a louder voice:

'Little children shall crawl in the ashes beside their mothers' corpses. At night men shall risk death by the sword to look for food among the ruins. Jackals shall fight over bones in the market-places where the old men used to talk in the evenings. Your daughters, swallowing their tears, shall play the cithara at the banquets of strangers, and the bravest of your sons shall bend their backs, galled by burdens too heavy to be borne!'

The people were reminded of the days of their exile and all the catastrophes of their history. These were the words of the ancient prophets which Jokanaan was hurling at them, like mighty blows, one after the other.

But then his voice became sweet, gentle, and melodious. He told of a deliverance to come, of wonders in the sky, of the new-born child putting his arm in the dragon's lair, of gold in the place of clay, of the desert blossoming like a rose.

'That which is valued now at sixty kikkars shall not cost an obol. Fountains of milk shall spring from the rocks, and men shall fall asleep in the wine-presses with their bellies full. When art Thou coming, Thou whom I await with hope? Already the peoples of the world kneel down before Thee, and Thy reign shall last for ever, Son of David!'

The Tetrarch started back, for the existence of a Son of David was an insult and a menace to him.

Jokanaan railed a him for his pretensions to kingship – 'There is no other king but the Lord!' – and attacked him for his gardens, his statues, and his ivory furniture, comparing him to the ungodly Ahab.

Antipas broke the little cord holding the seal which hung on his breast, and threw it into the pit, ordering him to be silent.

The voice replied:

'I will roar like a bear, bray like a wild ass, cry like a woman in labour. Your incest has already been punished, for God has afflicted you with the sterility of a mule!'

There was laughter at this, like the lapping of waves.

Vitellius persisted in staying there. In unemotional tones the interpreter repeated in the language of the Romans all the insults which Jokanaan was roaring out in his own. The Tetrarch and Herodias were forced to endure them twice over. He stood there panting, while she stared open-mouthed at the bottom of the pit.

The dreadful man threw his head back and, clutching the bars, pressed against them a face which looked like a mass of brushwood in which two live coals were glowing.

'Ah! It is you Jezebel! You took his heart with the creak of your slipper; you neighed like a mare; you set up your bed on the mountains to perform your sacrifices. But the Lord shall tear off your ear-rings, your purple robes, your linen veils, the bracelets on your arms, the rings on your toes, and the little golden crescents that tremble on your brow, your silver mirrors, your ostrich-feather fans, the mother-of-pearl pattens that increase your stature, the arrogance of your diamonds, the scents of your hair, the paint on your nails, all the artifices of your carnality;

and there shall not be pebbles enough for the stoning of your adultery!'

She looked around for someone to defend her. The Pharisees hypocritically lowered their eyes. The Sadducees looked the other way, for fear of offending the Proconsul. Antipas looked as if he were dying.

The voice grew louder and stronger, rolling and roaring like thunder, and as the mountains sent it back, it broke over Machaerus in repeated echoes.

'Grovel in the dust, daughter of Babylon! Grind your own meal! Take off your girdle, loosen your shoes, hitch up your clothes, and cross the rivers! Your shame shall be discovered, your infamy shall be seen, your sobs shall break your teeth! The Lord abhors the stench of your crimes! Accursed creature! Accursed creature! Die like a bitch!'

The trap-door shut and the cover fell back into place. Mannaëi would have gladly strangled Jokanaan.

Herodias disappeared. The Pharisees were shocked. Antipas, standing in their midst, tried to justify himself.

'Of course a man may marry his brother's wife,' replied Eleazar, 'but Herodias was not a widow, and moreover she had a child, which was what constituted the offence.'

'There you are mistaken', interposed the Sadducee Jonathas. 'The Law condemns such marriages but it does not absolutely forbid them.'

'All the same', said Antipas, 'people are most unfair to me, for when all is said and done, Absalom slept with his father's wives, Judah with his daughter-in-law, Ammon with his sister, and Lot with his daughters.'

Aulus, who had been asleep, reappeared at that moment. When the matter had been explained to him, he sided with the Tetrarch. No one, he said, should put himself out for the sake of such arrant nonsense, and he laughed uproariously at the priests' disapproval and Jokanaan's fury.

Herodias, who was half-way up the steps, turned round and said :

'You do wrong to laugh, my lord. He orders the people not to pay their taxes.'

'Is that true?' asked the publican straight away.

The replies were mainly in the affirmative, and the Tetrarch confirmed them.

It occurred to Vitellius that the prisoner might escape, and as Antipas seemed to be behaving suspiciously, he posted sentries at the gates, along the walls, and in the courtyard. Then he went off towards his rooms, accompanied by the deputations of priests. Each of these put forward its grievances, without mentioning the question of the High Priesthood. As they all beset him at once, he dismissed them.

Jonathas was just leaving him when he noticed Antipas standing in an embrasure, talking with a long-haired man dressed in white – an Essene; and he regretted having taken his side.

There was one thought from which the Tetrarch had derived some consolation. Jokanaan was no longer any concern of his, for the Romans had assumed responsibility for him. What a relief that was!

Just then Phanuel happened to be walking along the battlements. He called him over and, pointing to the soldiers, said :

'They are stronger than I am. I cannot set him free. It is not my fault.'

The courtyard was empty. The slaves were resting. Against the red sky which was setting the horizon ablaze the smallest upright objects stood out black. Antipas made out the saltworks at the far end of the Dead Sea, but he could no longer see the Arabs' tents. They must have gone, he thought. The moon was rising; a feeling of calm came over him.

Phanuel stood there, his chin sunk upon his breast, utterly dejected. At last he came out with what he had to say.

Since the beginning of the month he had been studying the sky every day before dawn, as the constellation of Perseus was then at its zenith. Agala was scarcely visible, Algol was not shining so brightly, and Mira Ceti had disappeared. From all this he augured the death of a man of importance that very night in Machaerus.

Who could it be? Vitellius was too well guarded. They were not going to execute Jokanaan. "It must be I!" thought the Tetrarch.

Perhaps the Arabs were going to come back? Or perhaps the Proconsul would find out about his dealings with the Parthians? The priests' escort was made up of hired assassins from Jerusalem, and they had daggers concealed in their clothing. As for Phanuel's prophetic skill, the Tetrarch had no doubts about that.

Then he thought of turning to Herodias for help. He hated her of course, but he knew that she would give him courage, and the spell she had laid on him in the past was not entirely broken.

When he entered her room, some cinnamon was smoking in a porphyry bowl, and powders, salves, filmy fabrics, and embroideries lighter than feathers were scattered about.

He made no mention of Phanuel's prediction, nor of his fear of the Jews and Arabs; she would have accused him of cowardice. He spoke only of the Romans: Vitellius had told him nothing of his military plans, and he suspected that he was a friend of Caius, with whom Agrippa was always consorting. If that were the case, he could look forward to being exiled, or even to having his throat cut.

With contemptuous kindliness Herodias tried to set his mind at rest, and finally took out of a little box a curious medal engraved with the profile of Tiberius. That, she said, was enough to make lictors turn pale and accusations melt away.

Antipas, moved and grateful, asked her how she had come by it.

'It was given to me', she replied.

From under a curtain in front of them a bare arm emerged, a charming young arm which might have been carved in ivory by Polyclitus. In an awkward yet graceful way it groped about in the air for a tunic left behind on a stool by the wall. An old woman drew the curtain aside and passed the tunic through.

A vague memory, which he could not quite place, crossed the Tetrarch's mind.

'Is that slave yours?'

'What does that matter to you?' answered Herodias.

3

THE guests filled the banqueting-hall to overflowing.

It had three aisles like a basilica, separated by pillars of sandal-wood, with bronze capitals covered with carvings. Two open-work galleries rested on these pillars, and a third in golden fili-gree projected in a curve at the back, facing a huge open arch at the other end of the hall.

Candelabra burning on the tables, which were set in rows the whole length of the building, formed sheaves of fire among the cups of painted earthenware, the copper dishes, the cubes of snow, and the piles of grapes; but because the ceiling was so high, their red glow seemed to fade away gradually, and points of light shone like stars between the branches. Through the opening of the great bay, torches could be seen on the terraces of the houses, for Antipas was feasting his friends, his people, and all those who had come to Machaerus.

Slaves as watchful as dogs moved about in felt sandals, carrying salvers.

The Proconsul's table stood on a dais with a sycamore floor, underneath the gilded balcony. Babylonian rugs were hung around it to form a kind of tent. Three ivory couches, one facing the hall and two at the sides, were occupied by Vitellius, his son, and Antipas, with the Proconsul on the left near the door, Aulus on the right, and the Tetrarch in the middle.

He was wearing a heavy black cloak whose texture was hidden under the colours applied to it; his cheeks were painted, his beard was trimmed in the shape of a fan, and his hair was dusted with blue powder and caught up in a jewelled diadem. Vitellius had kept on his purple shoulder-belt, which crossed his linen toga diagonally. Aulus was dressed in a robe of violet silk spangled with silver, whose sleeves he had had tied behind him. His ringlets were arranged in layers, and a sapphire necklace sparkled on his breast, which was white and fleshy like a woman's. Close beside him a very beautiful boy was sitting cross-legged on a mat, smiling all the time. Aulus had seen him in the kitchens and could not bear to be parted from him. Finding it difficult to remember his Chaldean name, he simply called him 'the Asiatic'. From time to time he stretched himself out on his couch, and then his bare feet dominated the entire assembly.

On his side were the priests and the Tetrarch's officers, some inhabitants of Jerusalem and the chief men of the Greek cities. Below the Proconsul were Marcellus and the publicans, some of the Tetrarch's friends, and notabilities from Cana, Ptolemais, and Jericho. Then, seated pell-mell, there were mountaineers from the Lebanon, Herod's old soldiers – twelve Thracians, one Gaul, and two Germans – gazelle-hunters, shepherds from Idumaea, the Sultan of Palmyra, and sailors from Ezion-geber. Each had in front of him a cake of soft paste to wipe his fingers on. Arms stretched out like vultures' necks to seize on olives, pistachio-nuts, and almonds. Every face looked radiant under its garland of flowers.

The Pharisees had spurned these as Roman obscenities, and they shuddered when they were sprinkled with galbanum and incense, a mixture reserved for the rites of the Temple. Aulus rubbed it into his armpits, and Antipas promised him a whole consignment of it, together with three basketfuls of the original balsam which had made Cleopatra cast covetous eyes on Palestine.

A captain from his garrison at Tiberias, who had just arrived, had positioned himself behind Antipas to inform him of some extraordinary events which had taken place. But the Tetrarch's attention was divided between the Proconsul and what was being said at the adjoining tables.

The guests there were talking about Jokanaan and people like him: Simon of Gitta, who cleansed sins with fire, and a certain Jesus.

'The worst of them all!' cried Eleazar. 'An infamous mountebank!'

Behind the Tetrarch a man stood up, as pale as the hem of his chlamys. He came down from the dais and shouted at the Pharisees:

'That is a lie! Jesus works miracles!'

Antipas would have liked to see some.

'You should have brought him with you', he said. 'Tell us something about them.'

Then the man told how he, Jacob, had gone to Capernaum to beg the Master to come and cure his sick daughter. The Master had said to him: 'Go back to your house; your daughter is cured.' And he had found her waiting for him on the threshold, having left her bed when the palace sun-dial marked the third hour, the very moment he had spoken to Jesus.

There was no denying, replied the Pharisees, that potent herbs and practices did exist. Here in Machaerus itself you could sometimes find the baaras plant which made men invulnerable. But to cure without seeing or touching the sick was impossible, unless Jesus made use of demons.

And the Tetrarch's friends, the chief men of Galilee, nodded their heads and said 'Yes, he must be using demons.'

Jacob, standing between their table and that of the priests, looked sad and haughty, but said nothing.

They called on him to speak.

'Justify his power!'

He bent his shoulders, and then, speaking quietly and slowly as if he were afraid of himself, he said:

'Then you do not realize that He is the Messiah?'

All the priests looked at each other askance, and Vitellius asked what the word meant. His interpreter hesitated for a moment before answering.

They gave that name to a liberator who would give them possession of all goods and dominion over all peoples. Some even maintained that two Messiahs were to be looked for. The first would be vanquished by Gog and Magog, demons of the north, but the other would exterminate the Prince of Evil, and for centuries they had been expecting him to arrive any minute.

The priests having consulted together, Eleazar spoke up.

To begin with, he said, the Messiah would be a son of David and not of a carpenter. Then, too, He would uphold the Law, whereas this Nazarene attacked it. And finally – and this was a more telling argument – He would be preceded by the coming of Elias.

'But Elias has come!' replied Jacob.

'Elias! Elias!' repeated the crowd down to the far end of the hall. All of them saw in imagination an old man with ravens flying above him, lightning setting fire to an altar, and idolatrous pontiffs thrown into raging torrents; while the women up in the galleries thought of the widow of Sarepta.

Above the clamour Jacob could be heard saying over and over again that he knew Elias. He had seen him, and the people had seen him too.

'His name?'

Then he cried at the top of his voice:

'Jokanaan!'

Antipas fell back as if he had been struck full in the chest. The Sadducees leapt upon Jacob. Eleazar went on shouting to gain a hearing. When silence had been restored, he threw his cloak about him and began putting questions like a judge.

'Seeing that the prophet is dead . . .'

Murmurs of disapproval interrupted him. It was generally believed that Elias had only disappeared.

He turned angrily on the crowd, and then went on with his interrogation.

'Do you think he has come to life again?'

'Why not?' said Jacob.

The Sadducees shrugged their shoulders. Jonathas opened his little eyes wide and gave a forced laugh. Nothing, he said, could be more ridiculous than to claim eternal life for the body. And for the Proconsul's benefit he recited this line from a contemporary poet:

Nec crescit; nec post mortem durare videtur.

But at that moment Aulus bent over the edge of his couch, his forehead bathed in sweat, his face green, his hands clasped to his stomach.

The Sadducees pretended to be deeply distressed (the next day the High Priesthood was restored to them); Antipas made a great show of concern; Vitellius remained unmoved. His anxiety was none the less very real, for if he lost his son he lost his fortune too.

Aulus had scarcely finished making himself vomit before he wanted to begin eating again.

'Give me some marble dust, some Naxos schist, some sea-water – anything! Or perhaps I ought to take a bath?'

He crunched a little snow, and then, after hesitating between a Commagene terrine and some pink ousels, he decided on pumpkins and honey. The Asiatic gazed at him in wonder, for this faculty for guzzling marked him out as a remarkable being sprung from a superior race.

While ox-kidneys were being served, together with dormice, nightingales, and minced meat wrapped in vine leaves, the priests discussed the problem of resurrection. Ammonius, a pupil of Philo the Platonist, thought they were stupid, and said so to some Greeks who were joking about oracles. Marcellus and Jacob had struck up acquaintance. The former was telling the latter of the happiness he had experienced on being baptized into Mithras, and Jacob was urging him to follow Jesus. Palm and tamarisk wines, the wines of Safed and Byblos, flowed from jars into bowls, from bowls into cups, from cups into gullets, and soon everyone was talking and exchanging confidences. Jacim, although a Jew, was no longer making any secret of the fact that he worshipped the planets. A merchant from Aphek was dazzling the nomads with a description of the marvels of the temple of Hierapolis, and they were asking how much a pilgrimage there would cost. A German who was nearly blind sang a hymn in praise of the Scandinavian promontory where the gods appeared with their faces bathed in light, while some people from Sichem refused to eat any turtle-doves, out of respect for the dove Azima.

Several of the guests stood talking in the middle of the hall, and the steam of their breath mingling with the smoke from the candelabra made a fog in the air. Phanuel went by close to the wall. He had just been studying the heavens again, but he did not go up to the Tetrarch for fear of being splashed with oil, which for the Essenes constituted a great pollution.

Suddenly someone was heard beating on the castle gate. It was now known that Jokanaan was a prisoner there. Men with torches were climbing up the path; others were swarming in a dark mass in the ravine; and from time to time they shouted: 'Jokanaan! Jokanaan!'

'He does nothing but stir up trouble', said Jonathas.

'No one will have any money left if he goes on', added the Pharisees.

And recriminations were heard on all sides:

'Protect us!'

'Make an end of him!'

'You are abandoning religion!'

'Ungodly as the Herods!'

'Less so than you!' retorted Antipas. 'It was my father who built your temple!'

Then the Pharisees, the sons of the proscripts, and the disciples of the Matathias charged the Tetrarch with his family's crimes.

They had egg-shaped heads, bristly beards, weak and evil-looking hands – or else snub noses, big round eyes, and the appearance of bulldogs. A dozen of them, scribes and priests' assistants who fed on what was left over from the burnt-offerings, rushed up to the edge of the dais and began threatening Antipas with their knives, while he harangued them and the Sadducees made a feeble show of defending him. He caught sight of Mannaëi and signalled to him to go away, for Vitellius was showing by his expression that none of this was any concern of his.

The Pharisees, who had stayed on their couches, worked themselves up into a demoniacal fury, smashing the plates in front of them. They had been served with wild-ass stew, a dish which

Maecenas loved but which they regarded as unclean. Aulus chaffed them about the ass's head, which they were supposed to hold in reverence, and made other sarcastic remarks about their aversion to the pig. No doubt this was because that lumpish animal had killed their Bacchus – and they were excessively fond of wine, as was shown by the discovery of a golden vine in the Temple.

The priests did not understand what he was saying. Phineas, a Galilean by birth, refused to translate it. At this his anger passed all bounds, especially as the Asiatic had taken fright and disappeared, and the meal was not to his liking, consisting as it did of commonplace dishes with insufficient seasoning. He calmed down, however, when he saw some Syrian sheep's tails, sheer bundles of fat.

The Jewish temperament seemed hideous to Vitellius. Their god could quite well be Moloch, whose altars he had come across beside the road; and he remembered what he had heard about the sacrifices of children and about the man they had mysteriously fattened up. As a Latin he was nauseated by their intolerance, their iconoclastic fury, their brutish obstinacy. He wanted to leave, but Aulus refused. With his robe let down to his thighs, he was lying behind a great pile of food, too gorged to eat any more, but stubbornly refusing to leave it.

The people grew more and more excited. They started discussing ways and means of obtaining their independence, and recalled Israel's glorious past; every one of her conquerors had been punished – Antigonus, Crassus, Varus . . .

'You scoundrels!' said the Proconsul – for he understood Syriac, and his interpreter's only function was to give him time to prepare his replies.

Antipas hurriedly took out the medal of the Emperor, and, trembling as he looked at it, he showed it to Vitellius with the image uppermost.

Suddenly the panels of the golden balcony were folded back, and in a blaze of tapers, surrounded by her slaves and festoons of anemones, Herodias appeared. On her head she wore an Assyrian mitre held in place by a chinstrap; her hair spread in ringlets over a scarlet peplum, which was slit down the length of the sleeves. With two stone monsters, like those which guard the treasury of the Atrides, flanking the door, she looked like Cybele standing between her lions. Holding a patera in her hand, she looked down from the balcony above Antipas and shouted:

'Long life to Caesar!'

This cry of homage was echoed by Vitellius, Antipas, and the priests.

But then there arose from the far end of the hall a hum of surprise and admiration. A girl had just come in.

Under a bluish veil which concealed her head and breasts, one could just make out the arch of her eyes, the chalcedonies in her ears, and the whiteness of her skin. A square of dove-coloured silk covered her shoulders and was fastened to her loins by a jewelled girdle. Her black trousers were spangled with mandrakes, and she moved with indolent ease, her little slippers of humming-birds' down tapping on the floor.

Going up on to the dais, she removed her veil. It was Herodias as she used to be in her youth. Then she began to dance.

Her feet flashed to and fro, to the music of a flute and a pair of castanets. Her rounded arms seemed to be beckoning someone who was forever fleeing from her. She ran after him, lighter than a butterfly, like an inquisitive Psyche or a wandering soul, always apparently on the point of fluttering away.

The castanets gave place to the funereal sound of the pipes: hope was followed by despondency. Her poses now suggested sighs, and her whole body was so languid that one could not tell whether she was mourning for a god or expiring in his embrace. With her eyes half-closed, she twisted her body backwards and forwards, making her belly rise and fall and her breasts quiver, while her face remained expressionless and her feet never stopped moving.

Vitellius compared her to Mnester, the mime. Aulus was vomiting again. The Tetrarch was lost in a dream and had forgotten about Herodias. He thought he saw her with the Sadducees, but the phantom vanished.

It was no phantom. She had had Salome, her daughter, brought up far from Machaerus, till the time came for the Tetrarch to fall in love with her. The idea was a good one: she felt sure of that now.

Next the girl depicted the frenzy of a love which demands satisfaction. She danced like the priestesses of the Indies, like the Nubian girls of the cataracts, like the bacchantes of Lydia. She twisted from side to side like a flower shaken by the wind. The jewels in her ears swung in the air, the silk on her back shimmered in the light, and from her arms, her feet, and her clothes there shot out invisible sparks which set the men on fire. A harp sang, and the crowd answered it with cheers. Without bending her knees, she opened her legs and leant over so low that her chin touched the floor. And the nomads inured to abstinence, the Roman soldiers skilled in debauchery, the avaricious publicans, and the old priests soured by controversy all sat there with their nostrils distended, quivering with desire.

Then she pirouetted madly round the Tetrarch's table, like the sorceresses' humming-top, and in a voice broken by sobs of passion, he cried to her:

'Come! Come!'

She went on spinning round, while the crowd roared and the dulcimers rang out as if they would burst. But the Tetrarch could be heard shouting above the din:

'Come! Come! You shall have Capernaum, the plain of Tiberias, my citadels, half my kingdom!'

She threw herself on her hands with her heels in the air, and in that position ran round the dais like a great beetle. Then she stopped abruptly.

Her neck and her spine were at right angles. The coloured sheaths about her legs hung down over her shoulders and on either side of her face to within a cubit of the ground. Her lips were painted, her eyebrows black, her eyes well-nigh terrifying, and the beads of sweat on her forehead looked like vapour on white marble.

She did not speak. They looked at one another.

There was a snapping of fingers in the balcony. She went up there, came down again, and lisping a little, said with a childish air:

'I want you to give me, in a dish, the head . . .' She had forgotten the name, but went on again, smiling: 'The head of Jokanaan!'

The Tetrarch sank back in horror.

He was bound by his word, and the people were waiting. But then he thought that if the death which had been predicted to him were inflicted on another, his own might be averted. If Jokanaan were really Elias, he would be able to avoid it; and if he were not, killing him was a matter of no importance.

Mannaëi was at his side and understood what was required of him. Vitellius called him back to give him the pass-word for the sentries guarding the pit.

Antipas felt relieved. In a moment it would all be over.

However, Mannaëi was far from quick about his work. And when he came back he was terribly distressed.

For forty years he had held the position of executioner. It was he who had drowned Aristobulus, strangled Alexander, burnt Matathias alive, beheaded Sohaemus, Pappus, Joseph, and

Antipater, and yet he did not dare kill Jokanaan. His teeth were chattering and he was trembling all over.

In front of the pit he had seen the Great Angel of the Samaritans, covered with eyes and brandishing an enormous sword, red and jagged like a flame. Two soldiers whom he had brought along as witnesses would bear him out.

They had seen nothing except a Jewish captain who had rushed at them and was now no more.

Herodias's anger poured forth in a torrent of coarse and bloody abuse. She broke her finger-nails on the lattice-work of the balcony, and the two carved lions seemed to be biting her shoulders and roaring with her.

Antipas copied her, and the priests, the soldiers, and the Pharisees followed suit, all shouting for vengeance, while the rest of the company were indignant that their pleasure should be delayed.

Mannaëi went out, hiding his face.

The guests thought he was taking even longer than he had the first time, and they began to get impatient.

Suddenly the sound of footsteps echoed along the corridors. The tension became unbearable.

The head came in – Mannaëi holding it by the hair at arm's length, proud of the applause which greeted him.

Putting it on a dish, he gave it to Salome.

She went nimbly up to the balcony, and a few minutes later the head was brought back by the old woman whom the Tetrarch had seen that morning on the roof of a house and later in Herodias's room.

He drew back to avoid seeing it. Vitellius gave it a cursory glance.

Mannaëi came down from the dais and showed it to the Roman captains, and then to all those who were dining on that side of the hall.

They examined it.

The sharp blade of the sword, striking downwards, had cut into the jaw. The corners of the mouth were drawn back in a grimace. There was blood, already clotted, splashed over the beard. The closed eyelids were as pale as shells, and rays of light fell on the face from the candelabra all around.

The head arrived at the priests' table. One of the Pharisees turned it over out of curiosity. Mannaëi set it upright again and placed it before Aulus, whom it awakened. Behind their lashes the dead eyes and the dull eyes seemed to be speaking to each other.

Then Mannaëi presented it to Antipas. Tears rolled down the Tetrarch's cheeks.

The torches went out; the guests departed; and soon no one was left in the hall but Antipas, his hands pressed against his temples, still gazing at the severed head, while Phanuel stood with outstretched arms in the middle of the great nave, murmuring prayers.

At the very moment that the sun rose, two men who had been sent out by Jokanaan some time before returned with the long-awaited reply.

They confided it to Phanuel, who received it with transports of delight.

Then he showed them the melancholy object on the dish among the remains of the banquet.

One of the men said to him:

'Take heart! He has gone down to the dead to proclaim the coming of Christ.'

Now at last the Essene understood the meaning of the words: 'If He is to wax, then I must wane.'

And taking Jokanaan's head, all three went off towards Galilee.

As it was very heavy, they each carried it in turn.

Some other books published by Penguins are
described on the following pages